To Matt

G. P. S. *for*
Living

Happy birthday and may God always be your G.P.S.

Garland Belgel

G. P. S. *for*
Living

GARLAND RAY PELZEL

XULON PRESS

Xulon Press
2301 Lucien Way #415
Maitland, FL 32751
407.339.4217
www.xulonpress.com

© 2019 by Garland Ray Pelzel

All rights reserved solely by the author. The author guarantees all contents are original and do not infringe upon the legal rights of any other person or work. No part of this book may be reproduced in any form without the permission of the author. The views expressed in this book are not necessarily those of the publisher.

Unless otherwise indicated, Scripture quotations taken from the Holy Bible, New International Version (NIV). Copyright © 1973, 1978, 1984, 2011 by Biblica, Inc.™. Used by permission. All rights reserved.

Although the author has made every effort to ensure the accuracy and completeness of abbreviations and information contained herein, he assumes no responsibility for errors, inaccuracies, omissions, or any inconsistency in this book. Any familiar slights of people, places or organizations are unintentional.

Printed in the United States of America.

ISBN-13: 978-1-54566-062-1

About the Author

Garland R. and Sue C. Pelzel are living out their retirement years in their home in Broken Arrow, Oklahoma. Their four grown children and twelve grandchildren live nearby. Garland is a retired Air Force Master Sergeant, with many medical conditions. He is diabetic and on dialysis three times a week. He is a disabled veteran and recently had his left leg amputated. He has also had a heart valve replacement and now has a pacemaker for his heart.

Sue is a retired gift store manager. She teaches Sunday school and two Bible study groups. They are both members of Will Rogers United Methodist Church in Tulsa, Oklahoma, and have been for nearly sixty years. Both have been on the Walk to Emmaus.

Garland has a Bachelor's degree in Business Administration from Northeastern State University in Tahlequah, Oklahoma. Sue graduated from business college in Oklahoma and later became their teacher/instructor.

G. P. S. for Living by Garland R. Pelzel
"G.P.S. for Living" (Global Positioning System)

This book is an autobiography of the life of Garland Ray Pelzel. He and his wife, Sue, are retired. They have traveled in all 50 U.S. States and also visited Canada, Mexico, Grand Cayman Island, Belize, the Bahamas, Germany, Switzerland, Austria, Italy, the Netherlands and Lichtenstein. Garland has also been in Thailand, South Vietnam, the Philippine Islands, Wake Island and Okinawa while in the U.S. Air Force.

The title of this book, "G.P.S. for Living," entails the author's excited summary of his life, giving both light and darkness, as he lived in the southwestern United States of America, during a dramatic period of time (horses to jets). A Global Positioning System (G.P.S.) is an electronic device included with most new cars to help the driver navigate, throughout some of our roads, as we travel. The Bible is our G.P.S. that gives us directions as we travel the roads of life.

In this book, you will recognize the times in Garland's life when he did not use God's G.P.S. that is available to everyone at all times.

DEDICATION

The Bible is our guide to wholesome and helpful living. Although this book contains an abundance of positive and negative aspects of how to live your life, the reader may find interesting anecdotes to guide them in their life. With great love and admiration, I hereby dedicate this book to my twelve living grandchildren (both biological and not): Kathryn, Jordan, Spencer, Mason, Tanner, Thomas, Summer Rose, Kenslie, Brady, Matthew, Dalton and Krysta.

THE AUTOBIOGRAPHY OF GARLAND RAY PELZEL

I was born August 30, 1936, in a farmhouse located just two miles northeast of Westphalia, Texas, a small Catholic community of German descendants, in the western part of Falls County. The county seat was, and still is, in Marlin, Texas. I was the third born of six to my parents, Johnnie Robert and Irene Minnie (Boettger) Pelzel. Both parents spoke the German language, but we kids spoke only English. Mom and Dad were married on May 11, 1930, in Waco, Texas (see photo #1)

The house we lived in was owned by my paternal grandparents, Henry and

Anna Pelzel, who lived nearby (photo #2). I do not remember anything about this house. I have seen many old photographs, which show it to be wood-framed, uninsulated and unpainted. It had an outdoor toilet that Grandpa and his family built years before. Their house was similar in size and structure.

My dad was the eighth of twelve children. My paternal grandparents' (Pelzel) house was wood-framed. The front door opened into the living room but most of the time, especially in the winter months, everyone hovered around the wood-burning heater-stove. Grandma did most of her cooking off of this stove, which was located in the kitchen-dining room of their house. This room also had a door that led to the outside toilet and barn. I remember playing in the upper lofts of the two-story barn, which stored hay and grain for the winter months for feeding the cattle, pigs, chickens, and guineas. I don't remember much more about their house except that Grandpa, after meals, would rest on the living room floor using a chair turned upside down to rest his back against, and that Grandma always had cooked prunes to eat. My grandfather, Heinrich Benjamin Pelzel, was born March 11, 1863, in Budigsdorf, Austria, now Krasikov, Czech Republic, and died July 4, 1847, in Rosebud, Texas, Fall County. Heinrich fathered twelve children. One died in infancy (see photos #2, 3 and 5). On November 9, 1897, my grandmother, Anna Schmid Pelzl (now spelled Pelzel), and Grandpa were married. Grandma was born August 17, 1877, in Zurich, Switzerland. She died March 3, 1965, in Rosebud, Texas. They are both buried in the Catholic Church cemetery in Westphalia, Texas. My maternal great-grandfather was Joseph Schmid, born, June 9, 1856, in Switzerland and he died March 30, 1921, in Westphalia, Texas. In 1847, he married Alberthie Huber Schmid. She was born

March 19, 1854, in Switzerland, and died April 1, 1931, in Westphalia, Texas (see photo #12).

My paternal great grandfather is Josef Pelzl, who was born August 10, 1820, in Budigsdorf, Moravia, Austria, now Czech Republic. Joseph married Anna Habermann from Kleintriebendorf, Sudetenland, Austria. Anna was born on July 2, 1825. Joseph and Anna married in 1847. They had seven children, all born in Austria. My grandfather Heinrich, Henry, was one of them. Josef died April 13, 1908, and Anna died February 13, 1905. They both died near Westphalia, Texas and both rest in the Catholic Church cemetery in Westphalia, Texas.

While my maternal grandparents lived in Lott, Texas until Grandpa died in 1948, they rented and lived in an upstairs apartment in a building owned by the Catholic Church next door. The lower part of this building was utilized by the Catholic Church's Sunday School classes. My grandparents rented the entire second story and used stairs to get to and from their living quarters. At the top of the stairs to the left was a large bedroom with one double-sized bed, sewing machine and a lot of other stuff. To the right of the stairs was the living room, which had a coal burning heater, sitting chairs, and another double-sized bed utilized by both of my grandparents. From the living room to the north was a very large kitchen and dining room. The cook stove was kerosene operated.

Before Grandpa was bedridden with asthma, he cooked. Off from this kitchen, to the east, led to a very large bathroom, which extended to the stairs, and the other direction led to a tin floor patio with rails. Also, from the bathroom to the east, was another large bedroom which had four more double beds.

Downstairs, out back, was a wooden walkway leading to three outhouses and to the coal shed. Grandpa purchased coal by bulk-block and they had to break it by hammer to bring it upstairs to burn. Uncle Robert received a large splinter in his bare feet walking on the wooded walkway.

Grandpa, Hugo Carl Boettger, was born September 29, 1883, in Black Jack Springs, Texas. This town was near FR 609, twelve miles southwest of LaGrange in southwestern Fayette County. The community, named for the nearby clear springs and Blackjack oak trees, was settled in the mid-1930s by Anglo pioneers. Grandpa died September 30, 1948, at his home in Lott, Texas from severe asthma. He is buried in Clover Hill Cemetery in Lott, Texas, near his son, Roy A. Boettger, who was killed in Italy on July 26, 1944, WWII. (See photo #11)

Grandma, Lydia Marie Zoch Boettger, was born July 5, 1890, near Serbin, Texas in Lee County. She died July 18, 1982, at age ninety-two in Rosebud, Texas. She is buried beside her husband in Clover Hill Cemetery in Lott, Texas.

My great grandfather, Gottlieb Zoch, was born February 26, 1859, in Sprewitz, Prussia (Germany), where he was baptized in the Lutheran Church and attended school there. In 1869, he came to the U.S. with his parents. He lived in Fayette County, Texas for seventy-five years. He died November 13, 1944, at his home near Warda, Texas. He was confirmed by Rev. John Kilian at Serbin, Texas on April 6, 1873. In 1881, he was married to Maria Domaschk and the union was blessed with twelve children. A surviving daughter, Lydia Marie Boettger, is my grandmother. Two of his grandchildren have given their lives in the present war, one of which was my Uncle Roy A. Boettger.

My great grandmother, Maria Domaschk Zoch, was born March 9, 1860, in Reichwaldo Prussia (Germany). She and my great grandfather were married in 1881. She died November 5, 1941, at their home near Warda, Texas. (See photo# 11)

My maternal grandparents were Hugo Carl and Lydia Maria (Zoch) Boettger. They were both born in America, and both spoke German and English. They were both buried in Clover Hill Cemetery in Lott, Texas, as are my parents. Grandpa Hugo Boettger had a brother named Adolph, and his wife's name was Sig. They had one daughter named Johnnie Marie. She was a registered nurse who died young from T.B. They used to live on the outskirts of Godley, Texas, near Cleveland. My maternal great grandparents were Gottlieb and Maria (Domaschk) Zoch. They had twelve children and are both buried in the Lutheran Church Cemetery in Warda, Fayette County, Texas. My other maternal great grandparents were Julius August Boettger, who married Minnie Schnier. Little is known about him, except that he was born in Germany, he married my great grandmother Minnie Schnier Boettger on August 24, 1875. Minnie was born in Germany on February 20,

1847, and died December 14, 1918, in Leroy, Texas. Minnie arrived in the U.S. in 1853, from Germany. Minnie died from Pneumonia.

Dr. B. A. Jansing, from Westphalia, was the attending physician who came the two miles by horseback to assist in my delivery. Until I was nineteen years old, we celebrated my birthday on August 31st. Then, I obtained a birth certificate from the county courthouse in Marlin. It showed that my birthday was recorded to be August 30th. Mom said that the court clerk, B. F. Smith, recorded the date incorrectly. But with no proof, other than her word, my birthday has since been celebrated on August 30th. When I was fourteen, I obtained a Social Security card, and those records showed the August 31st birth date. It wasn't until 1998, when I applied for Social Security benefits, at the age of 62, that the error was finally corrected.

In the '30s when I was born, almost everyone in that part of the country relied on farming to make a living. Dad was a farmer, raising cotton, corn, maize, sugar cane, hay, vegetables, and anything else he could think of to grow. Mom was a housewife, as well as a farmer, and because of her skill and determination, we always had something to eat.

From this farmhouse, where I lived the first two years of my life, I've heard many stories of Dad making whiskey to sell to his friends. He hid his still in the fields until someone spilled the beans, and the IRS came and destroyed his equipment. Fortunately, he didn't go to jail. He always blamed my uncle, Walter Boettger, Mom's brother, for telling the IRS. But Uncle Walter denied it, saying that he always loved drinking Dad's whiskey.

When I was past two years old, the family moved to nearby Travis, to live in another farmhouse belonging to my grandparents. This was a much better house than the former one. The property joined Dad's Uncle Ernst Schmid, Grandma Pelzel's brother, whose extended family was largely uneducated. Although this house was larger, like the other one, it was unpainted and uninsulated. And it was all open under the house. Like all the places we lived, until I left home at age nineteen, it was heated by wood. Cutting, sawing, and hauling wood for the stove was one of regular chores. First, we had to cut down the trees, often miles from home, and trim off all the smaller branches. Then we hauled them home with horses pulling them, later we used a tractor. Sometimes, we cut them into manageable pieces by two-man-pulled cross saw. Dad had a rear-wheel car axle. On one end of the axle, there was attached a large round saw blade, and on the other end was a pulley to attach a belt from a tractor. Before we had a tractor (1947), we would back our family car with one wheel elevated and against the pulley. With the other wheels blocked off, put the car in gear, and the elevated wheel would turn the shaft, and we would saw firewood to fit the one stove we had to heat the house during cold weather. The differential in the rear car axle allows one wheel to be steady when the other is turning. This homemade saw saved us from a lot of hard work. We could saw enough wood in three hours to last all winter.

I mentioned that this house was open all underneath, so that I could play under the house. But often, I crawled under the house to escape danger or punishment. My uncle, Ben Pelzel, was in the Army during WWII and would come by for a visit in his uniform. He agitated me by pinching me hard on the legs. I would escape his presence by crawling under the house, where I sometimes stayed until he left the house.

Our drinking water came from a deep, spring-fed well located closer to the barn than the house. We drew water by the bucket-full for the house, chickens, and sometimes for the livestock: cows, horses, mules and pigs. One time, a cat fell in the well and drowned, and caused the water to be undrinkable for about a day. We had to draw out all the contaminated water by the bucket-full, until it was almost dry and new fresh spring water refilled it, and everything was okay. We put a cover over the well to prevent another such occurrence.

We dug a storm cellar and stored our canned commodities there. We used it one time when a bad thunderstorm came through. It rained so hard, the water between the storm cellar and the house was waist deep on my older brother, when he returned to the house for flashlights.

In the early '40s, when my older brother, Dalton, was about eight years old, he came down with infantile paralysis. He eventually recovered, and I remember Mom and Dad teaching him how to walk again, which was a long, slow process. Dad made him a set of parallel bars to assist in his recovery.

I mentioned earlier about Uncle Ernst Schmid and his family living on the adjacent farm, just north of our farm. If you walked the mile to their house, you would cross over Black Bridge, that went over this large creek, that went through their farm. We often went to their house by cutting across the field and crossing the creek. Sometimes it was low or sometimes not running water. We fished out of this creek a lot and sometimes saw huge, hard-shell snapping turtles. Our older siblings and cousins always put fear in our minds whenever we saw these turtles, by telling us that if one of the snappers bit us, they wouldn't turn loose until it thundered.

We often visited the Schmid family at their house. They had twins about two years older than I was. They were not identical twins. One was larger than the other, so we called them Big Boy and Little Boy. They had many other brothers and sisters. One of the older sisters was born with a birth defect and she drooled constantly. She was in charge of us younger kids one time, and she caught us peeing through a hole in the floor of the house, and she scolded us good! The house was always filthy and cluttered. Uncle Ernst dipped snuff and spit on everything. He often got drunk and tried to destroy everything in his path. The whole family often escaped his destructive drunkenness by coming to our house.

When I was about three years old, my parents gave me a tricycle for Christmas. I rode that tricycle day and night. After the first year, the rubber tires wore out and Dad replaced them with iron wheels.

During this time period, we had Mexican neighbors to our south, and had a Mexican school house just north of our house, before the Black Bridge. They were all good neighbors and helped us out a lot. During hog-killing time in the winter, the Mexican neighbors often helped us butcher. Dad would pay them by giving them the hog head, the intestines, chitterlings, the tail, and the feet, and some of the liver. They thought they were overpaid, so they would make hot tamales and give us several dozen. Good stuff!

We lived on the corner of a gravel topped road, but often the mail carrier would deliver the mail on horseback, because at least half of his route was on dirt roads, which became mud when it rained.

In those days, if you had an automobile and couldn't repair it, you just junked it. We had this junked car parked behind the chicken house, next to a cluster of cane poles. There were always chickens under the car, and in the cane poles in search of shade. This also happened to be my playground. One day Mom had just received a mail order from the Sears catalog. I tried on these brand-new pants that I was supposed to wear to our grandparent's house later that day. I went back out to play and as I crawled through the old junked car, I heard this ripping sound. Yep! I had torn a large L-shaped hole in my brand-new pants! Mom really cussed me out good.

While I'm on the subject of punishment, let me tell you of the one lifetime spanking that I got from my Dad. I was about four years old and Dad was working on the motor of our family car—a 1934 Model A Ford. A nickel coin dropped from the breast pocket of Dad's overalls onto the ground. I saw the coin lying on the ground under the car and I grabbed it, claiming it was mine. "Finders Keepers." Not! Dad said it was his and he took it away from me. I put up such a fuss, hollering, yelling, and crying that Dad spanked my butt. I broke away from him, ran about thirty yards, and called him a, "shit-ass." He ran after me, caught me, and spanked me again. I ran again, about fifty yards this time, and called him a, "shit ass," again. He ran after me, again caught me, and spanked me. This time I broke away and ran even further and called him the same name again. Ah! Success!

Finally, he didn't come after me, so I kept running all the way down to the fields, still crying. I stayed gone more than half the day, sulking, and thinking about all my problems. I finally went home and everyone went about their business as though nothing had happened.

Most of the physical discipline I received while growing up came from Mother. If she didn't have a broom handy to swat me—brooms seldom hurt—but they make a lot of noise, she would grab anything she could find to whip me. I remember one time when I agitated her, she was using a butcher knife for something and as I ran from her she threw the knife at me and hit my left upper thigh. It gave me about a half-inch wound. I fell into the next room and stayed out of her reach for about half an hour. She never checked on me and when I told her later that I was wounded, she didn't believe me. She just thought I had hurt myself under the iron bed frame. I got no sympathy from her.

Most of my parents' discipline came in the form of loud, vulgar cursing. I was always embarrassed when Mom and Dad used profane language around friends, relatives, or just anyone they talked to. Each of them had only about a fifth-grade education. Mom attended Live Oak country school, three miles west of Lott, Texas. Dad attended Vinson country school, three miles east of Westphalia, Texas, at Poverty Flats. Name probably obtained after a Texas tornado destroyed the school and farm houses nearby.

When I was five years old, in 1941, my brother John Allen was born. Mother had the baby in our home, with our family physician. Dr. Swepston came from the Rosebud, Texas Hospital.

In later years, we kids witnessed some furious fights between Mom and Dad with a lot of shouting and cursing. Mom even used the broom on Dad. But as I recall, Dad only shielded himself from her attacks and never hit her back.

Mom was heavier and really strong from all the hard, physical labor of farm living. Dad was handicapped in that he could not close his left hand. He was involved in an automobile accident as a passenger that cut the leaders in his left hand. This happened back in 1931, and doctors didn't have the skills they do today. In this condition, just think about the things you couldn't do or would be hard to do: milk a cow, pick cotton with both hands, roll a home-made cigarette, and on and on.

So, at age six, in 1942, I started school, in elementary school, in Travis, Texas.

We walked the mile to and from school on gravel roads. In the first grade, my teacher's name was Mrs. Stublefield. In the second grade, my teacher's name was Mrs. Snodgrass. In the middle of my second-grade year, 1943, we moved from Travis to New Salem, which was about six miles to the east.

Dad bought some underdeveloped, barren land one mile east of the township community of New Salem, Texas. He got it cheap, but it was really more than he wanted to deal with. First, we had to build a house, a barn, and all the other sheds. Dad did all this with used lumber, with Mom and all us kids helping. My older brother, Dalton, was now twelve years old, and was involved with a lot of the hard work. We soon moved into our small bungalow-style house. Our relatives were amazed at Dad's skills and abilities. Next, we started digging a well next to the house. Dalton did the digging from within the well, and the rest of us drew up the buckets of dirt with a rope and pulley. After about four feet, we hit solid sand. So, we stopped digging because of the danger from the sand, that could easily cave in and bury one of us. We sealed off the bottom with concrete and bricked it on to the top of the earth. It was now a cistern. Water is obtained from rains and guttered from the roof into the cistern.

This supply of water was seldom enough. We often hauled water from our widowed neighbor, Hattie Willie, who was about ninety-years old. We would fill a fifty-five-gallon barrel with water and haul it home on a wooden sled pulled by horses and mules. A barrel would last us a week.

The next big project was digging a pond that would hold water for all our livestock. There were two creeks leading through our farm, but their water wouldn't last through the hot Texas summers. We only had horses and mules for farming. Dad and Dalton dug a large stock pond using a mule-pulled hand scraper. This scraper would normally pick up a yard of dirt at one time, so you can imagine how long it took to dig this tank. Originally, it was half-sized and the rains filled it up. Later we dug another trench beside the filled pond and this left a middle ridge between the two ponds. In later years, the ridge diminished and the two ponds became one large pond. In this pond is where I first learned to swim. Dalton would throw me into deep water and this technique taught me to "sink or swim." We stocked this pond with fish, and they grew fast. A lot of my play time involved fishing at the tank, swimming, or crawfishing from the creek nearby. Our bait for crawfishing was bacon. There was always plenty in the smokehouse.

This story must also include the bad times, because that's what life is all about—good times and bad times. Dad and Dalton came home one day by horse and wagon from the previous home place in Travis (six miles). Dad was all beat up. His face was beaten and bloody. He looked worse than Sylvester Stallone in Rocky I, II and III. Before we had moved from the house owned by the grandparents in Travis, Dad had replaced most of the window screens. Dad had said for many years that Jim owed Mom and Dad for helping them pick cotton one year. Dad's sister, Julie, and husband, Jim Zaleski, were now living in this house. I'm sure Dad knew that any improvements permanently attached to rented or borrowed property are supposed to remain on the property. Since our new house in New Salem did not yet have screens, Dad tried to take the screens from the house in Travis. Uncle Jim, who was big and strong, stopped him.

Dalton, as an eyewitness, would only say that Uncle Jim had beaten the hell out of Dad. Uncle Jim probably thought he deserved the beating. Dad had devilish ideas sometimes.

Dad's family was all Catholic, but he left the church when he married Mom because she was a Lutheran. Dad was twenty-two and Mom was fifteen when they married in 1930. They never sought a relationship with God or went to church until later years.

My brother Dalton was friends with the Mitchell family, who lived next to the Canterbury family farm, on the Travis to Cedar Springs Road. When I was about eight years old, Dalton and I walked over to the Mitchell's, about two miles. While Windall Mitchell and Dalton dug up mud clods below a culvert, I tried to do the same next to their culvert. A rain storm came and we were forced to take shelter in the Mitchell's barn. We were all wet, tired, and hungry. When the rain slowed down, Windall went into his parents' house and came back with a tray of biscuits and honey. Boy was that really good! We got our strength back and we walked back home.

So now, it was time to start the second half of my second-grade school year.

New Salem was, again, one mile away. The three of us walked the sometimes-muddy road. I was the only one in the second grade of that country school. My teacher's name was Mrs. Matty. During this school year, Mrs. Matty had us participate in an old, Negro minstrel play. Boy, was that black charcoal hard to get off our faces! She also taught about six kids in the first grade. So, as it turned out, I became a teacher's aide for first graders. As a result, I learned very little in the second grade, including cursive writing, I could only print. But I was still promoted to the third grade, and when school started in the fall, I was the only one in the third grade. Now, the school was only teaching grades two, three, and four, with only one teacher, Mrs. Vickers. Her daughter, Connie, was in the fourth grade with my sister, Carol. Dalton had to take another route to catch the bus to school in Lott.

Mrs. Vickers was not very nice, and she was very impatient and wouldn't take the time to teach me as the lone third grader, since she also had to teach the other two grades. So, she talked to my parents and I ended up repeating the second grade.

More trouble...Alfred, was a little Mexican boy who also went to school with us. He lived two miles from school, which was a mile past our house. Carol and I picked on Alfred so much that we were reprimanded by both Mom and Mrs.

Vickers. It got so bad that Alfred's mom would walk to school with him, and Mrs. Vickers would let him leave 30 minutes early to get ahead of us. We would sometimes run and catch up with him just so we could pick on him some more. That earned more scolding from the teacher. But I didn't care. She had pissed me off by putting me back in the second grade.

One day, I was climbing on the shed that was attached to the barn. I was wearing overalls. I lost my grip and fell. As I was falling, my pants caught on a nail and I tore them beyond repair. When I fell, I landed in a big pile of fresh cow manure. So, with the big tear and the nasty cow manure, I crawled out of the overalls and buried them. They were later found by Mom and I caught more hell.

Another thing that Carol and I did going home from school, was to steal fruit from the neighbor's house. We had to walk by the Roy Lloyd family farm. At that time, they had two kids—Donald, age five and Kay, age three. When we were walking by, we could see Roy and his wife picking cotton. I would entertain Donald and Kay to distract them, and Carol would sneak into the house and steal fruit for both of us from the pantry. She would hide it in her dress or her coat. After we got on down the road, we would have ourselves a little after-school snack. During those days, we never had store-bought fruit at home, and boy, was it good! I have since asked for and received forgiveness for that sin. By the way, in later years, Donald Lloyd made a career of the Air Force. We were stationed together in U-Tapao, Satahip, Thailand in 1967.

After that school year, New Salem closed the school. So, in 1945, the three of us walked the mile and caught the bus to Lott ISO. I was then in the third grade. My teacher was Mrs. Clara Ed Schiller, who was my class mate, Lee Edward Romain's aunt. Our mail box was located where we caught the school bus. After school, we would bring any mail that we have home with us, along with Hattie Willie's mail. When school was not in session, we often made dry runs one mile there, and one mile back.

A year before this, my brother Larry Roy was born. Mom went to her parent's home in Lott to have the baby. She named Larry after her brother, my uncle Roy Boettger, who was killed, in Italy, in WWII. Mom's other brother, Robert Boettger, was wounded the same year in Italy. Uncle Roy's daughter, Martha Ann Boettger, my cousin, got me my first date with my future wife, Sue Carolyn Looper, in 1961, in Tulsa, Oklahoma.

WWII was still in full force. FDR had to ration many commodities like gasoline, sugar, cooking oil, and lube oil. We fished a lot in the Brazos River. Sometimes we sold some of the fish when we had an abundance. Since we were rationed on cooking oil, we baked our fish in the oven. Our cook stove was operated with kerosene, as was our lighting. We often went to bed when the chickens took to their roost.

The falls on the Brazos near Carter Munch was a favorite fishing place, and so was the brush hole near Pool Creek. The brush hole was often hard to get to because of the swamp-like, muddy road. We often got stuck, and sometimes had to leave the car or truck until the next day. So, we had to walk a half a mile with all our gear to fish. One time Dad, Dalton, and I went to the river (brush hole) by covered wagon and horses. It was about eight miles. one way. We caught a lot of fish, and Mom, the little kids, and several relatives joined us by driving another route and crossing a deep creek to get to our camp by foot. Mom got stuck in some mud, up to her knees, in the middle of the creek. It took three grown men to pull her out, but I really think that she laughed her way out. She thought it was SO funny. After the party was all over and the company left, we laid down to relax, when we heard this cowbell go *ding-a-ling*. That was a sign that a fish was on the trot line. We pulled off a large twelve-pound gasper. It swallowed the hook, which meant it would soon die. We made a decision to break camp and head home. With the horses running part of the time, we made it home before dark.

Times got really bad on the farm. We raised tomatoes and cotton for

income...and corn, other grains, and a full garden to live on, as well as beef and pork. Dad had to go to Waco and got a job on the MKT Railroad. He worked, lived in a hotel room, cooked his own food, and on weekends, he came home to help us with the farming. We would drive to Waco on Friday and bring Dad home and on Sunday afternoon, we would drive him to Travis and he would catch a train to Waco.

We made friends with the Dentons, who lived up the road closer to Cedar Springs, Texas. Mr. Denton looked like Will Rogers, from Oklahoma. Their two sons were part of the WWII Army. The oldest Denton boy, while stationed in Georgia, married a girl with a real southern drawl. I really enjoyed listening to her talk. The younger Denton, Jack, never married. Jack often made himself available to drive us in our car to bring Dad home on weekends. Sunday dinners at the Denton's were fabulous.

Sometime during this period, we obtained a bicycle to share between us three older siblings. When it was my turn to ride it, I quickly learned how to ride, but not until I'd had the handlebars jammed into my ribs. The tires were always flat because of all the burrs and stickers around.

During the week, there was a do-si-do in the Cedar Springs School gym that Mom would take us to. Square dancing and cake walks were a lot of fun, and we got our fill of sweet stuff, including girls.

In 1946, after the war was over, Dad's job with MKT railroad ended, and he came back home to full-time farming. But that didn't last. He got a construction job building the mile-long bridge on highway 77 in Cameron, Texas, over Little River. He made a campus shell out of an old pickup bed. He parked it on the south bank of Little River, lived in it, and fished a lot until he got time off to come home. In the year 2006, the bridge was destroyed and a new one was being constructed.

Also during 1946, when I was ten years old, my eyes started giving me trouble. I had to make weekly trips to Rosebud Hospital, and Dr. Swepston treated my eyes. He always had to dilate my eyes and the procedure was painful. The final thing he always did was put some kind of salve in my eyes. Mom had to lead me back to the car like a blind person. It always took a half a day to clear before I could see again. A lot of improvements in medical science have made this procedure painless. I know, because I have annual checkups with the VA (see Photo #4—is the building in Rosebud, Texas, that was the hospital). That is where I had my weekly eye treatments in 1946. That is where my sister, Carol, had her tonsils removed and, in 1955, gave birth to her first-born, Dennis Montgomery. Just a month earlier, our sister, Raedene, was born. Also, in 1960, it's where I brought my younger brother, Larry, to get a tetanus shot right, after I shot him with a twelve-gauge shotgun. Yeah, Uncle Walter, John, Larry, and I were dove hunting just south of the Wilburg farm. There was an old barn, and I shot at some doves flying toward the barn. Larry was hunting on the other side of the barn, completely out of my sight. One BB from the number-six shotgun shell bounced off the tin roof and ricocheted down and hit Larry. The BB went through his left shoulder muscle, leaving a one-inch gap from the entrance point to the exit. It didn't even bleed.

On September 1, 1946, my Uncle Buster Ballard was murdered at his residence at 1507 McKell Street, Dallas, Texas. Buster, by our standards, was wealthy. When he came to visit, he would always give us kids candy and a toy. If we *weren't* home, he would turn over every bed in the house and still leave us candy and toys. He took us to the first zoo I had ever been to in Dallas. He smoked cigars, and this smell was left everywhere he went. We were in good standing with Buster's parents. The Ballards (seen in photo #5) lived in Waco and we visited them often, probably because Buster and Freda first lived in Waco after they married. Their oldest daughter, Joyce was born in Waco.

Anyway, back to Buster, he owned a clothing manufacturing company in Dallas. He always brought his cash receipts home with him. One night at 2 a.m., a couple came to his door and demanded money. The man had a gun. Buster opened the screen, pushed his three curious daughters out of harm's way, turned to strike the man and was shot in the heart. He made it half-way to his bedroom where he kept a gun and fell dead in the hall. The couple was caught by the police, and the guy only got fifteen years jail time. Buster was forty-one years old when he died. Buster's death, Eugene Lynch Ballard, will live in infamy.

We prepared to leave for Dallas on Saturday, the funeral was on Sunday. First, I had to go to Rosebud for eye treatments, and then we had to go by and pick up Uncle Ike, Dad's youngest brother. It was a rainy day. Our car was a 1938, four-door Ford. Dad, Dalton and Uncle Ike sat in the front seat. Mom, me, Carol, John, and Larry were in the back. Halfway to Dallas, Uncle Ike had an epileptic seizure. He came out of WWII with this condition and spent a lot of time in VA hospitals. This really scared me. He had convulsions, lost consciousness, foamed at the mouth, kicked, and quivered. The odor was unbearable. Dad stopped the car, dipped his handkerchief in rainwater in the ditch, wiped Ike's face, and cooled his forehead. After about fifteen minutes, he regained consciousness and we continued on to Dallas. And no one, including us kids, said one word until we got to Aunt Freda's house.

After we arrived at the Ballard's house, they showed us the bullet hole in the screen and just how far Uncle Buster got down the hall before he died. Then, all of us kids had to sleep on pallets on the floor—it was a very ghostly night, considering all the events that had taken place that day. On Sunday, the funeral was the largest I had ever seen, both then and now.

In 1947, Dad sold the New Salem farm and we purchased the former Hal Storey estate. It was just six miles northwest of Lott, and two miles south of Durango. It consisted of 125 acres, some pasture, a stock pond, cool spring-fed well water, a large older home, plenty of outbuildings, and a barn. It was accessible by gravel road. We also now had electric power.

Dad also bought a used "B" model John Deere tractor, so we now had two ways to farm the land. When I was about fourteen years old, I used to help Dad with farming, using mules. Even though we had the tractor, we used both. I would have the mules running this two-row stalk cutter. In farming, at different times, when you couldn't turn the cattle to graze the old corn stalks, you cut the stalks with a stalk-cutter so that you could plow the land and get it ready for other crops. I found it interesting to know just how smart some animals are. I could merely voice the command, "Giddy-up," and the mules would start pulling. I could say, "Whoa," and they stopped. We had this blind mule that was a very dependable, hard worker. After a half-day's work, sometimes all day, I would un-harness this mule at the barn, and watch it make its way through the small trees to the stock pond, over a hundred yards away to get a drink of water. It would bump into a limb and change its path, but for the most part, it found its way every time. Now, we still walked one mile—one way, to catch the school bus, and it took one hour to make all the stops. One more good thing was that our mailbox was now right out in front of the house, and you could see the mail carrier coming a mile away.

While Dalton was still at home, everyone had left to go somewhere, leaving just the two of us there. We were assigned the task of hauling bales of hay to store in the barn. Dalton would hand me the bales from the outside, and I would catch them and stack them inside the hot barn. I was smaller, probably around twelve years old at the time, and I got tired very quickly and couldn't keep up with the pace Dalton set. I got mad at him—this happened a lot—and ran from the barn towards the house. He picked up a brick and threw it at me. It bounced off the ground and hit me on the forehead. I faked it by falling on the ground and just laid there very still. I was bleeding, but not badly. After a while, Dalton decided he couldn't do all the work alone, so he came over and checked on me. He took me into the house and washed my wound, apologized to me, both us got a drink of water from the well, and both of us returned to finish our jobs.

On another occasion, during a cold winter day, when all you could do was sit around the wood-burning stove all day to keep warm, Dalton held the door to the living room shut so I couldn't get back in to get warm. I kicked in the bottom of the door and ruined it beyond repair. What do parents do when the kids are uncontrollable? They curse you and run you to the barn to shuck and shell corn. This is a never-ending task and we could never seem to get ahead of doing it.

On still another occasion, Dalton agitated me and then ran from me. So, I picked up a long piece of wood and threw it at him. We were on the long front porch which had large windows on it and when he ducked, the stick broke out two large window panes. Guess what? Back to the barn to shuck and shell corn.

On one weekend, when I was about fifteen, I was left all alone to do all the chores: milk cows, feed the chickens, corn-shuck and shell it, first, feed the hogs corn on the cob, water or slop the hogs, and fill the chicken trough with water for the chickens, cats, and dogs. I was given the old international pickup to drive. It was Saturday. I got all the chores done early, bathed in the clear stock pond, dressed, and was ready to go to town (Lott). The old pickup wouldn't start, and in those days, we didn't have the trusty old battery charger. So, I got on my bicycle and took off. It was six miles to Lott, three miles on a dirt road and three miles on the highway. It took me eighteen minutes to get to Lott.

I had a chain and I locked the bike to a utility post. I had money, and I made my usual purchases of candy and ice cream before going to the movie. After the show, it was time for more snacks, and a visit with friends before the open-air boxing matches began. After the boxing matches, the midnight movie began. It was over about midnight. So, I got on my bike and headed home. I met five cars with their blinding lights on the highway. There was enough moonlight to see the road and, again, I made it home in eighteen minutes. That is about twenty miles an hour.

In 1949, Dalton graduated from Lott High School. He excelled in sports, especially football. He immediately left home and joined the Marine Corps. That same fall, I was in the seventh grade. I played football for the first time. I didn't know diddly-squat about football. In later years, I excelled just like my older brother.

During the war years, we spent a lot of time picking wild berries, grapes, and pecans to supplement our food supply. Some of the biggest and best berries came from the river bank at the brush hole. Nearly every time we went berry picking, Mom and I would come in contact with poison ivy and break out in a rash. Mom suffered the most, because it spread so quickly over her body. It would take a week of daily applications of calamine lotion to get rid of it.

Dad taught me how to skillfully hunt rabbit and squirrels with a 22-gauge rifle. Many, many times I would go hunting and bring back rabbits. Mom would fry them and we had them for meals. Sometimes, we would grind the meat and make chili, especially with big jackrabbits. Dad could spot a sitting rabbit one-hundred yards away. My eyesight was never that good.

Some of my memory stuff includes two FFA pins for vocational agriculture, dog tags after joining the Air Force in 1955, with my name, serial number, AF18488756, T55 for tetanus shot and blood count A-Positive, at the Waco Baylor District meet—for first place—in the 880-yard run in 1954, second place in the mile run in 1953, second place in the mile relay in 1954, third place in the mile relay in 1953, second place in the 880-yard run in 1955, and third place in the shot put in 1955.

During the growing-up days of my life, I recall we raised tomatoes for a living. Dad and Uncle Jim Zaleski, Spanish speaker, would travel to Falfurrias, Texas to buy tomato plants, and bring back oranges for eating. We would punch holes in the soil with a broom handle, place the tomato plants in the holes, pour water, and cover the roots with dirt. We would have to water the plants for several days before they started growing on their own. We didn't have insecticide spray in those days, so we had to pick caterpillars off the plants daily, to keep them growing. Later, we picked the tomatoes green, and took them to market to sell.

One year, we raised turkeys to sell. When the turkeys were growing up, if we didn't feed them thoroughly, they would leave home to find insects to nourish their bodies. We would have to go off in the evening to herd them home for protection from wild animals. Sometimes they would wander two miles from home.

During that same time period, we had this small dog as a pet. She was my hunting dog. Often, rabbits would escape my aim and go into holes to hide. This small dog would go into the hole after them and drag them out and I would finish killing them. The best eating rabbit is the swamp rabbit. The swamp rabbit is larger than a cotton tail. We only found swamp rabbits on Grandpa Pelzel's place near Westphalia, and near the Brazos River at the brush hole.

In 1950, Mom and Dad, Carol, and I would hire out to hoe other people's cotton fields for four dollars each day. Combined, we made enough to buy our first electric refrigerator. Before that, our icebox was exactly that—we bought blocks of ice, placed it in an insulated cabinet to keep food cool. Of course, you had to be able to afford to buy the ice in town, then hurry home with it before it melted. The City of Lott had an ice house on Main Street. Chicken Smith was the owner. Most of the time he was there at the ice house, but he often made home deliveries. If he was gone, you could help yourself and his sign read, "Help yourself and pay me when you see me. But don't go blind!" So, it was really wonderful when we got the fridge and could have ice anytime we wanted it. And, it was even better, when Mom made ice cream and froze it in ice trays.

While growing up, water was always at a premium. Before leaving the house to tackle such jobs as wood-cutting, corn and cotton field hoeing, hauling hay, fishing, etc., we would go to the well, fill our jugs, that had been wrapped in cotton cloth, and pour water over the cloth to keep the drinking water cool all day. Sometimes our work area was close to a well, across the creek. We didn't have a pulley rig on this well, so we used a wire, tied to a bucket and hand-pulled it up. Often there would be red fire ants alive on top of the water bucket, so we would have to rake them off first before drinking from the bucket. When pulling cotton near this well, Dad would send one of my younger brothers to get a bucket of cool fresh water. Mom would drink first, then Dad. When it got to me, Dad's tobacco breath was all over the bucket and I didn't like it at all!

During the year 1950, there were many children from families nearby that shared the same bus stop corner, to go to school at both Westphalia and Lott school districts. Families such as the Pelzels,

Wilburgs, Rebitskies, Boswanks, Gregors, Weavers, and the Harolds. Many of our ancestors share some of the same hard-times stories. I want the readers to know about our past, so that they will fully understand just how wonderfully blessed we are, to live in a country that has a wealth of freedom and security. The Weaver children rode the same bus to school with us beginning in 1950. Here is their story:

Irmgard, Ilse, and Horst Kunkel became the adopted children of Mr. and Mrs. Verner Weaver. There German names were given the English translation and became known as Erma, Elsie and Horest Weaver. They arrived at Love Field, in Dallas, Texas on May 9, 1950, the first children allowed a legal exit from Red Germany. They had left behind their past and hoped to find a new and more pleasant life with their relatives/adoptive parents in America. Frail and frightened, not knowing a word of English, they were anxious to find out about their new home.

Erma, Elsie and Horest were born to Leo and Freida Kunkel, a well-to-do farm family. Their farm home was, in what was the Polish Corridor—a strip of land taken from Germany in 1919 and given to Poland as a route to the Baltic seaport. Their home was white brick with a large flower garden in front. The post office was across the street. Their father had servants who did the farm work and their children often played together.

After Hitler's blitz into Poland, Leo Kunkel became a German citizen by Nazi decree, and was registered with the German Army on October 24, 1942, at the age of forty-seven. Later, he was informed, that his personal property now belonged to the Germans.

Meanwhile, the war had progressed far from the Kunkel farm into Soviet Russia. But, by January of 1945, began its victory march across Poland into Germany. Leo Kunkel and his family decided to stay on their farm. They had lived under the Polish flag, and then the German flag, and would chance a life under the Russian flag.

That was a mistake. One night, some soldiers came to the door and ordered Mr. Kunkel to come with them. He never returned. After about a week's wait, the children and their mother packed everything into a wagon. Not very far down the road, they were stopped by soldiers, who took their wagon and they were taken to a concentration camp. There were a lot of people there. The women, and children, and the old men were in one section and all the other men were in another section.

Some trucks were parked across the way, and Erma, Elsie and Horest saw their father on one of the trucks. They called and waved to him, but the guards would not let them go to him. The guard also refused to let their mother talk to their dad. In a few minutes, the trucks left and they never saw their daddy again. Freida Kunkel and her three children, then nine, eight and five years old, began a life of agony in concentration camps. The food was usually weak soup. When there was meat, their mother gave her portion to her three children.

They were hauled from one camp to another in railroad box cars. People were tightly packed inside.

Many got sick and many died. From time to time, the train would stop and push the dead bodies out. If the train stopped overnight, they would sleep in bombed-out buildings.

On Christmas Day, 1946, the Russians released Freida Kunkel and her three children. They had no place to go but found refuge in a barn in the Russian zone of occupied Germany near the city of Griefwald, on the Baltic Sea. Freida Kunkel was suffering from malnutrition and soon contracted pneumonia. Besides her food, she had also given her clothing to her children.

Early in March of 1947, Freida was moved to a hospital at Griefwald, by the Red Cross. The children were cared for by different farmers in the community. Seeing that her health was failing, she wrote to her cousin, Paula Gettel, who lived in the American zone city of Wiesbaden, West Germany. She wrote this note: "Help my children. Help them to be freed from this land." A week later, Freida Kunkel died.

Irmgard, Ilse, and Horst were placed in an orphanage in Griefwald, by the Red Cross. Shortly afterward, they received a letter informing them that their father had died in a work camp in Staline, Russia in 1946. The only physical memento the children had of their father was a small, poorly made, metal crucifix. Their mother had carried it with her through the years of hardship.

When she died, it passed on to Erma.

Remembering the plea of Freida Kunkel for her children, Gustav and Paula Gettel were determined to carry out her wish. After receiving letters from Paula Gettel, Mr. and Mrs. Weaver began thinking seriously of adopting the three Kunkel children. They sent packages of food and clothing to them. Twenty-eight years married, the Weavers were childless, and these children were their own blood-kin. Mrs. Weaver's father, August Gregor, was a brother of the children's grandmother. So, after deciding to adopt the children, they learned they would need certificates of death for both of the children's parents. The communists would not even tell them where Leo Kunkel was buried. But Gustav Gettel had many friends in the Russian zone, and he remembered his pledge to his cousin. Leo Kunkel's brother-in-law, a man named Otto Hubert, had been in the Salino work camp with Leo. Gustav found Otto in the city of Jena, and on January 12, 1948, Otto made this state in writing:

"I hereby swear to the following: As a former inhabitant of Warthland, along with many other Germans, among them was the farmer, Leo Kunkel of Gruntowitz, who was known to me personally. I was brought to a work camp in Staline, Russia. In this camp Leo Kunkel died either in May or June 1946. I cannot give you the exact time of death."

Gustav brought the document back to West Germany and sent it to Verner Weaver. The death certificate of Freida Kunkel was dated February 10, 1948, nearly a year after her death. She died in a hospital at Griefwald at 9:00 a.m. on March 27, 1947. Her maiden name was Freida Dusterhofts, the daughter of Landwir Emil Dusterhofts and Elisabeth Gregor Dusterhofts.

With these documents found, the children were able to leave the Russian zone. After three years of delays, disappointments, and many anxieties, the Weavers received a letter from Lucie Gottel, the daughter of Gustav and Paula on April 28, 1950:

"Today I share with you news that we have just received a letter from Frankfort. On May 4th, I am to pick up the visas for Irmgard, Ilse and Horst. We are so happy that at last everything has worked out after all. I shall now write the airlines that I am going to get the visas May the fourth so they can make reservations right away. Now everything will go quickly. When I know the exact date of the children's flight, I will write immediately, or better still send a telegram. Other than this, there is nothing new, but I have told you the most important thing, haven't I?"

The children's plane fare alone, would cost the Weavers 1,136.75 dollars. A small cost for three wonderful children they so badly wanted. Irmgard, Ilse, and Horst boarded an American Stratocruiser, number N-90944, Flight 175 for New York at 5:30 p.m. on May 7, 1950. They were forced to land in Ireland for the night after one engine lost power. They arrived at Love Field in Dallas, Texas on Tuesday, May 9 at 5:25 p.m. Frightened and knowing no English, they stepped off the plane to be greeted by their new parents. They had reached their destination safely.

The children brought with them a note from Paula Gottel, asking the Weavers to let her know if the three youngsters had arrived safely. Before Mrs. Weaver's letter reached Weisbaden, Gustav Gottel had died, his pledge fulfilled.

In the fall, the children were enrolled in Westphalia schools. With the help of their teachers and their parents, they were able to speak English within six weeks of study. All through high school they were excellent students and won many honors. Perhaps the biggest day of their lives came on November 11, 1954, when each became a citizen of the United Sates. They had their greatest dream fulfilled and have continued as grateful citizens of America. They lived on the Weaver farm and learned all the chores common to farm life.

Erma married Henry Roessler in 1956 and lives near Tours in McLennan County. Elsie married Ray Johnson in 1957, and now lives in San Antonio, Texas. Horest married Bernice Ranley in 1966 and he and his family reside near the home of his mother and father near Westphalia, Texas. *The Weaver family story was reprinted, by permission from <u>The History of Westo, Halig, Texas</u> book published by the Church of the Visitation in July 1979.*

In 1950, my brother Dalton and his friend Windell Mitchell were in the Korean War in the U.S. Marine Corp. They decided to start a relationship between Windell's sister, Margarette, and Dalton. They set it up for Margarette to spend several weeks with us—Dalton's family—on the farm, so that she could become acquainted to our way of life. My sister

Carol was given a reprieve from her farm chores to accommodate Margarette during her visit. It was corn-pulling time, and normally Carol and I were assigned the two rows of corn that was run over by the wagon while Dad took two rows to the left and Mom took two rows to the right. The two rows that were driven over by the wagon were the hardest to pull since they were laying on the ground. During this visitation time, I had to take care of both rows on the ground. I was further handicapped, because I tore a large area on the bottom of my foot from climbing a chinaberry tree with nails sticking out. Needless to say, I didn't approve of this relationship. Besides, it never materialized anyway, because the two found other partners.

In 1951, when my sister, Carol Faye, finished tenth grade, she talked Mom and Dad into letting her go out on her own. She was fed up with farm life. It was too hard on her. I hated to have her leave, because that made my workload even heavier. She went to Waco and became a bar hop.

During the winter months we found rats in our hay barn. With a club and some tough pet dogs, I killed about fifty rats in our barn, but a lot of them escaped our mauling. As I would turn the hay bales over, I would club some of them, but often missed and hit the dogs instead. They must have wondered about their decision to help. But those dogs could kill a rat in the blink of an eye. We often shot the rats with a .22 rifle as they climbed high in the rafters. But the bullet holes in the tin roof soon made it counter-productive.

To supplement our food supply during the lean winter months, I often caught or shot pigeons living on our barn. I often built boxes for them to nest in and reproduce. Dad taught me how to build a bird trap to catch field larks to eat. We would watch the traps from inside the warm house at the living room window, and only went outdoors to retrieve a captured bird and pick all the feathers, before coming back in the house.

Also, in the winter months, we sat around the old wood burner to keep warm. This was in the dining room and in later years, this was where the TV was located. We would crack and eat pecans for snacks. When we kids started getting too loud, Mom and Dad would run us out of the house to the barn. We always had corn to shuck and shell. The cows ate the shucks, the hogs ate the corn on the cob, and the chickens got the shelled corn. This was a never-ending job—365 days a year.

Dad would often be netting a fish net during those cold, winter months. Catching fish in a gill net was legal as long as the mesh was at least three inches. never was interested in learning how to do this, but I enjoyed taking fish from the net in the Brazos River.

One of my childhood chores, in the evening, was to walk down to the pasture, which was sometimes as far as a mile, and herd the milk cows home. Sometimes, especially during the winter, they came home on their own because we fed them hay from the barn. Sometimes, when I walked behind the cows as they went single file on the trail, I had to watch out because a cow can walk and poop at the same time. Being too close, you could get splattered with cow manure. Some of the cows allowed me to ride on their backs part of the way home.

While growing up, I hated the time period of my birthday, August 30th. It was always cotton-picking time, just another hard day's work for a farmer's son. Generally, I always had a birthday cake and enjoyed eating my share of the sweet homemade cake that Mom always made.

It was also in 1950 that Dalton was sent to Korea. He was part of the Marine division located in the Chosin Reservoir, near the Manchurian border. They were surrounded by North Korean and Chinese forces. Dalton was wounded in the hand and suffered frost-bitten feet. He spent a lot of hospital time in Japan before coming home after the Korean War. Historically, he was part of the "Frozen Chosin."

It was during this time period that God spoke to my mother. He said, "Irene, whether you believe it or not, I have set an appointed time with destiny which cannot be evaded or postponed. If you'll choose My way, I'll guarantee you much happiness and eternal life. If not, then you'll go to hell where you'll suffer much fire and gnashing of teeth."

Although I never actually lived in Lott, Texas, I've always claimed it was my hometown. After all, I did graduate from Lott High School. Lott was founded and established in 1890, by Uriah Lott. He formed the first railroad through that area to help bring in trade from all directions, in Central Falls County.

So, we began going to church and Sunday school at the Methodist church in Lott, Texas. We were accepted and became members, and the family, including Dad, was baptized by being sprinkled. After this, the language in our household improved. Not as much cursing. We even began to have the preacher over for Sunday dinner—mashed potatoes and gravy, fresh English peas, and fried chicken. On the farm, to have fried chicken took a lot of time and effort. First we had to catch the young fryers. That could take up to an hour. Then we had to boil water, pull the heads off, and let them bleed out, soak them in hot water, pick off all the feathers, singe off the feathers over the burners on the cook stove, gut them, cut them into pieces, roll them in flour mixed with spices, heat the grease, then fry them. Where is KFC when you need them?

In the seventh grade, I just got a taste of the fundamentals of football. I remember playing a night game and, afterward, six of us had to walk all the way home. The few cars that came by wouldn't stop to pick up six guys. I lived the farthest from town. A football game followed by a six-mile walk will really take it out of you. I was tired!

During high school, on a cold rainy night, we had a basketball game. After the game, I rode the three highway miles with Henry Earl Pomycal because he lived out that way. I had to walk the other three miles on muddy roads. It was ninety-nine percent dark and it was hard to stay on the road. The mud with clay stuck to my shoes making each step heavier and harder. After I finally got home, it took me another hour to clean up my shoes and set them to dry to wear the following morning.

From the eighth grade on, I excelled in football. I was on the "A" team all four years in high school. My ego got a big boost in the field house during a freshman game when the coach scolded the team, we were losing, and said that I was the only player that was hustling. I made *All District* in my Junior and Senior years. Also, my senior year, I was selected as Most Valuable Lineman in the district. I boxed and won the high school Regional Middle Weight Championship my junior year. I also excelled in track, baseball, softball and volleyball. I played basketball, but was never very good at it. In later years, I played football for the Air Force while I was stationed in Houston.

In early high school, I dated a girl who was the daughter of the Church of Christ's Preacher. I attended this church a few times during this courtship. There was no music allowed in the church. My classmate, Joy Beth Evans, also attended this church. Her dad was our superintendent of schools. A lot of the girls I dated were Baptist, so I was familiar with that religion. Another church experience was in 1957, when I had a *one-date fling* with a girl who was a Jehovah's Witness. I thought it was hilarious watching those people roll around, shouting, and singing.

When I was in the fourth grade in the Lott, Texas school system, Bubba Odenbach and I got into a fight on the old wooden bleachers of the football field. I think I won. In later years, about the sixth grade, a bully, oversized student, pissed Bubba and I off. I held the bully's arms while Bubba pounded his fist into the bully's face. Some upper classmates broke up the fight. In high school, another bully pissed Bubba and I off, so again I held his arms behind him while Bubba pounded his fist into his face. The Principal caught us in the act and, while in his office, he asked us if we would use boxing gloves and one-on-one. We both said yes. It never happened. We left scot-free and nothing more ever happened.

An interesting anecdote:

On May 11, 1953, a tornado hit downtown Waco. Three women from Lott were killed when a building collapsed on the car they were in, as they were leaving town after work. It flattened the car, so one can only imagine what it did to their bodies. It was a category-three tornado with winds up to 130 mph. Carol lived in Waco, and we didn't hear anything from her. After three days, we were allowed to drive into parts of the city, where we finally found Carol, safe and sound.

In the fall of 1953, I hitchhiked to Waco to visit Carol. I stayed in her apartment. I had this date with Peggy Collier, from Waco High School. Shirley Asher, a Lott High School classmate, had a date with Peggy's brother. The four of us went to a movie and later to a snack shop. I was wearing old hand-me-down pants, and the pocket where I had all my money, broken loose in the movie and I lost all I had except for one dime. At the snack shop, I told them that I didn't want anything. I was so embarrassed. I unhappily finished the day and the next day I used the dime to ride the bus to the traffic circle and hitchhiked back to Lott. Mom was there at church, so I had a ride home from there. I have never revealed this "Most Embarrassing Moment" to anyone ever before.

During high school, during the winter months, some of us boys would go to the city lake and swim naked in the hot water in the large pool that was getting ready to be pumped to the city's water tower. The water was hot because, when it came out of the artesian supply, it was that way.

I got into trouble in school in the fall of my senior year. Three of us on the football team had an open weekend. So, after school on Thursday, we jumped in Bubba's 1931 Model A Ford and headed toward Alto, Texas. Our favorite coach, Johnny McClendon, was transferred there. We saw their game and came on back home. Monday, we three were reprimanded and threatened with expulsion. The football team stood up for us. Only five guys suited up for practice. The staff reconsidered and said, "Okay, we won't expel you." So, we all suited up and made it to practice late. We stayed after school that one day as punishment.

Superintendent Evans had to take us home. Bubba lived in town, Billy Floyd lived close to Cedar Springs, and I lived near Durango. When our report cards came out we all had a "U" in conduct. That was the extent of our punishment.

In high school, FFA (Future Farmers of America) was an easy course but taught us many necessary situations for healthful living. With home projects, in the three years I took Ag, I earned an extra 1 credit toward graduation. One year I raised egg-producing chickens. Another year I won a calf in the Houston Fat Stock Show and Rodeo in the calf scramble. Another year I raised a heifer. Other projects were rope making, and I built a brooder house for raising baby chicks during the winter months. Mom and Dad used that brooder house for many years after I left home. Our Ag class went on a lot of field trips to castrate calves and hogs. I recall one nasty, rainy day trip when we went to castrate hogs. We came away smelling like hog mess. I went to our athletic field house and put on some cleaner clothes, but for the most part, we still stunk. Our next class was with Mrs. Lillian Romain. Her son, Lee Edward, was a part of our Ag group. When Mrs. Romain came into our classroom, she said, "What's that I smell?" All she got from us guys was laughter, but later one of the girls told her privately what she was smelling. At noon, she sent her son home to change clothes.

The senior class of Lott High School attended the Centex Fair in Waco in 1955. This motorcycle rider called me over to the side and asked me if I would ride with him inside this small arena. I said yes, and this promoted interest for the class to pay to see me ride with him. I found it interesting to learn that he took off gradually and began our ride around and around. I felt as though I was riding on a flat surface.

My senior year was the best year of my school experience. I had a steady girlfriend named Eda Davenport. She was a Baptist and I went to church with her and her family. Her family drove a new 1955 Ford, blue and white with a lot of chrome. It really was a beauty of a car! I messed up and played around on Eda and was unfaithful to her. She dropped me when she found out. I broke her heart.

Another side note:

It was in 1954 that my family bought our first television. We thought any of the three channels in black white were good. In today's programming, 2017, I often can't find anything interesting with 300 channels in color.

Dad followed the weather forecasting and would pick a cold, winter day to kill and butcher a hog. The chore would take all day. After you build a fire under the blackened, steel pot filled with water, and it begins to boil, it's time to kill the hog. Dad would have me shoot the hog in the head with my .22 rifle, using long bullets. The .22 short bullets would not kill the hog. After shooting the hog, Dad would slit the hog's throat to bleed it thoroughly. Then we would have to lift the hog and put it on a slide pulled by mules or a tractor to get it near our work area, which was near the pot of hot water. We would cover the hog with burlap sacks and pour the water over them. The burlap sacks helped retain the heat of the water long enough to tenderize the hair, so we could begin the hard task of scraping the hair off the hog. We used a sharp butcher knife to scrape the hair. You had to use both hands. Lay the knife over the area and pull in one direction to scrape it.

Next, we would cut into the hind leg muscles and hook a single tree from a cultivator plow and pull the hog up a tree limb, using a pulley and rope. Next, we would cut around the tail and rectum area and tie it off, thus preventing any hog mess from coming out everywhere. Then, as you cut the hog open from his tail to his head, you would catch all the guts in a tub. This included the liver, heart and kidneys. After clearing this, you would cut the entire head off the hog. Next, you did a final hot water cleansing to remove the remaining blood. By using a meat hand saw, we cut out the entire backbone section from the tail to the neck. Now, it's time to unhook each side from the hanging single tree and place on a butchering table to do the rest of the work.

Picking a cold day helped preserve the meat, reduce the possibility of flies, and made cutting the meat much easier. We continued to use the black pot with hot water by throwing in the liver, heart and kidneys, the pig feet and most of the head to make head cheese and sausage. While this was cooking, we often forked up a piece, added salt and pepper, and had a snack. Mom was always assigned the task of cleaning the small and large intestines and stomach to use in sausage making. Dad did most of the butchering. All four leg portions went for hams. The backbone was for soup bones. The rib sections went for bacon. All of us kids had the chore of cutting lean meat into small enough pieces to use in the hand turned meat grinder. We trimmed the fat from the meat to use in making lard.

The final use of the black pot for the day was cooking the fat for lard. Grinding the lean meat was a hard and tiresome job. Grinding the already-cooked meat for head sausage was easier. We used the same grinder to press the meat for making sausage. As the meat fills the intestines, it might remind someone of a colonoscopy. Yuck!

Dad would cure the hams, soup bones, and bacon in a barrel of salt and sugar water for about ten days, and then hang them, along with all the sausage, in the smokehouse. The smokehouse was a tin-covered building with dirt floors. We would build a fire in a large pot or pan, and used green hickory that would put off smoke. We kept this smoke going night and day as much as we could for about two weeks. When we were hungry, we would go into the smokehouse and break off a piece of sausage and eat it. It didn't need any further cooking. Mom would do the meat seasoning, but you would know later that Dad always added more spices—like father, like son.

In May 2011, we started construction of a combination smokehouse, tool and slaughter house, and work room building at the lake house in Wagoner, Oklahoma. The building is twenty-two feet by fourteen feet on a concrete slab. It has a fireplace-barbecue, smoke room, and benches for tools. This is an ideal addition to our lake house. Our son-in-law brought two four-wheelers and the kids just love them.

After graduation, I worked a few jobs. I made spending money by boxing on Saturday nights in Lott. Rolla Will Hailey, who later became Judge Hailey, ran a dry goods store, and his wife ran the movie theater. Rolla Will got the other merchants in Lott to pool their money and pay people to box in an open-air arena. I was one of the guys who boxed. This drew all kinds of people from Central Texas to enjoy the free entertainment. There would be three or four bouts every Saturday night. He scheduled the fights after the first movie showing. After the fights, he would announce the midnight show at the movie.

In October 1955, I made the decision to join the Air Force. The eleven weeks of training at Lackland AFB in San Antonio was challenging and strenuous. I was given the career field of my choice which was *personnel*. I was assigned to a radar station in Houma, Louisiana, which was located sixty miles south west of New Orleans. This station had about 150 people assigned. Personnel and Administration shared offices in the Orderly Room, along with the First Sergeant, Adjutant, and Commander. We often had to clean the Orderly Room. One day, I was sweeping the floor around the Commander's desk, when I accidentally knocked a trophy off and broke it. I was so embarrassed, but he was forgiving and compassionate. SSgt. Robinson was an Administrative Specialist working in the Orderly Room. I was a new Airman Third Class and remembering proper behavior learned in training, I called him, "Sir." He didn't think I should call him, "Sir." Many years later in 1971 while assigned at Tinker AFB, OK, there was Robinson, still a SSgt., but now I was a MSgt. He thought that he should call me, "Sir."

I didn't like the looks of the Methodist church in Houma. It reminded me of a monastery. So, I joined with some other guys from the base, and went to the First Baptist Church in Houma. I would later join and be baptized, by submersion, in the church. The pastor's name was Leon Hyatt and he looked like Jack Lord from Hawaii Five-O. The church, Sunday School, and BTU (Baptist Training Union) were all great fellowship. We had about twenty in our youth group. We had a great leader and had parties, fishing trips, and other appropriate social functions. I even water skied, for the first time in my life, at one of the lake outings.

There were canals all over Houma. You could travel by car or boat. We also swam in the Intracoastal Canal, as well as fished. A New York friend and I hitchhiked to Port Arthur to visit my uncles, Walter and Robert, and their families. His name was Boardman Smith, and he was from Brooklyn, New York.

From that time on, I hitchhiked home a lot. It was 500 miles. I was in uniform and that made it easy to catch a ride. It was ten hours driving time, and I could usually make it in eleven to twelve hours, when I hitchhiked. On the downside, Southern Louisiana was full of "queers." You wouldn't believe all their techniques of seduction. Thankfully, God was watching over me. The first clue that I had when I was picked up by one of them, was for them to put their right arm out behind my neck and touch me. We had a guy from Lott who was homosexual. He even graduated from Lott High School. One night he chose me to seduce, but it didn't work. He has since died from Aids. It is my belief that the devastation and destruction in Louisiana from hurricanes in 1957 and 2005, and others in between, are a judgment from God for their wickedness, much as He did with Sodom and Gomorrah in chapter nineteen, Genesis.

In 1956, I purchased my first automobile. It was a 1947 Studebaker. It
wasn't much, but good enough to drive around Houma with a date. I borrowed money, and bought a set of wedding rings, and became engaged to Janie Beville. I met her in Sunday school and we went to BTU together every Sunday. Our relationship wasn't going too well, and then the wedding band was stolen from my footlocker. I'd left the locker open while taking a shower. I was convinced the thief was a black guy in our barracks named Archie S. Smith (ASS). Anyway, I
broke off the engagement with Janie and sulked because of my poverty. I never seemed to have any money until I made E-7, MSgt. in 1969. In 1957 I sold my Studebaker after I almost crashed in it, when the brakes went out, while I was driving it on Highway 90 in downtown Houma. I dodged oncoming cars by driving in the far lane, and turning the corner, stopping on the curb near the Bijou Theater. Later, I drove it back to the barracks using the hand brake and low gear. After that, my second car was a 1951 Fleetwood Chevy. And then in 1958, I traded the Chevy in for a 1954

Pontiac, in Gretna, a New Orleans, suburb on the west bank of the big river.

Also, in 1958, I became engaged to Frances Jacqueline Bergeron from Houma. We also met in Sunday school at the First Baptist Church. She was seventeen years old and between her Junior and Senior years of high school. Dad helped me get a loan from a bank in Rosebud, Texas, to buy rings, and pay some on the wedding. So, we planned the wedding after Jackie's mom, Clarice, said that we could live with them after we got married. I was only an A2C, E-3, in the AF and made about 200 dollars a month at that time. Air Force policy is that you receive counseling from an Air Force chaplain prior to getting married if you are below the rank of SSgt., ES. I received prayer and counseling.

So, on July 18, 1958, we were married by the Reverend Leon Hyatt, in the First Baptist Church of Houma, Louisiana. Surprisingly, guests from Texas were Mom and Dad, my sister Raedene, three and a half, sister Carol and her husband Bill Jim, my grandmother Boettger, Uncle Walter and his wife Ollie.

We honeymooned in Texas. We had Grandma Boettger's house in Lott while she was visiting Walter in Port Arthur. This may have been a mistake because on the first day, Jackie witnessed Mom's temper when she got angry at Billy Jim for drinking on the entire trip to Louisiana and ran him off from the farm. After our return to Houma, I packed my bag and went with our softball team to play at MacDill AFB, Tampa Bay, Florida. That was a long-hot, humid trip. One-way travel time took twelve hours.

Upon our return from Florida, you would think that we settled down to married life. We "unsettled" down to married life. Jackie didn't allow me to be the head of the household. We were living in her parent's house, so everything remained, "Mom this" and, "Mom that". We argued, she didn't want to be married anymore. I was kicked out. I had no choice but to go back to the base to live. Jackie's brother James got married shortly after we did. He and his wife, Nell, asked us to live in part of their unpainted, rented house. It was cheap, so we got some furniture on the time plan, and moved in. This place was only three blocks from her parent's house and she still spent more time there than she did with me. The rest of the time she was in school—it was her senior year.

To this day, I can't remember why we couldn't get along with each other. We called Rev. Hyatt on many occasions and he talked with us and Clarice. He realized that Clarice had a dominate hold on her daughter, but it seemed hopeless. One day I came home from work, and all the furniture was gone. Only my clothes and personal stuff was left and scattered all over the house. I had to gather my things, and while doing this, Clarice and Jackie drove up to Nell's side of the house. I ran out toward Clarice, as if I were going to smash in her face, but I faked it and did not touch her. I left with all my belongings after I found out they had called the furniture company to come out and repossess the furniture.

That night, as I moved back into the barracks at the base, the Officer of the Day called me into his office in the operations building. He told me someone from the Sheriff's office was coming out to pick me up for attacking my mother-in-law and causing her bodily harm. I told the OD what happened and he said not to worry and go peacefully with the officers. He had already called the First Sergeant and my Personnel Officer, second Lt. O'Nesky from Oklahoma. The officers came to the base and took me to the county jail. The jail keeper took me in and, for the next hour, he was processing me in to be jailed. That included the following: emptying your pockets, accounting for every dime, taking finger prints, and mug shots. Before they could put me in a cell, the First Sergeant and Personnel Officer came and asked me if I was ready to go. I asked where and they said back to the base. So the jailer unprocessed me by giving back every dime that was in my pockets, including my wedding ring, and we left. Therefore, I was never actually jailed. So we went back to the base, and we all had to brief the Acting Base Commander, Capt. Franklyn James, as to what was happening. By then it was midnight and they'd all left. I went to a phone booth and called Clarice to let her know I was not in jail and hung up. The next day, everyone knew that I had called Clarice. She probably called the police and asked for protection because I was out and on the loose. The police had talked to Neil and she told them I had not touched Clarice. She had picked up a stick, hit her arm and told police I had harmed her. So, the police dropped the case against me that wasn't justified. I am reminded of one of the Ten Commandments, "You shall not give false testimony against your neighbor (or son-in-law)" Deut. 5:20.

At one time, Jackie thought that Rev. Leon Hyatt was taking my side in the matter. So, we joined the Southeast Baptist Church with Pastor Hebert (pronounced A-Bear). It was a smaller church and I really didn't like it. One day, Brother Hebert and Brother Hyatt called me in for counseling. Before it was all over, I felt so embarrassed, because they asked to lead off in prayer. Now, at this time in my life, every week I pray with the Pastor and I'm not embarrassed but blessed.

On March 1, 1959, something good finally happened in my life. I was promoted to AlC, E-4. My superiors thought my life would be better if I transferred from Houma. So, I was transferred 300 miles away to Thomasville AFS, Alabama, which is one-hundred miles due north of Mobile, Alabama. Jackie refused to go with me. She stayed with her momma and finished school.

Moneywise, I was getting more pay, but I still owed on a loan from the Rosebud Bank, for the ring and the wedding. So, I applied for early re-enlistment. My original separation date was October '59. When you take an, "early out," to re-enlist, you can't sell your accrued leave time. So, I only received the reenlistment bonus. I sent the money home to pay off the loan and I still had enough to apply to a down-payment on my next car. So, I went to Mobile and traded by 1954 Pontiac in for a 1957 Chevy.

In May 1959, I took a thirty-day re-enlistment leave and went home to Texas. More tragedy. I had gone hunting and killed a bunch of rabbits and had the grill out ready to charcoal the meat. The grill fire was not doing well, so my brother, Larry, got a can of gasoline. Picture this in your mind: John Allen is standing on the far left of the grill. I was right of him, Raedene, now age four, was on my right and Larry, now age fourteen, was on the far right. As he prepared to throw the gas on the fire, little Raedene started forward and John Allen shouted, "Watch out!" just as Larry slung the gas. The shout startled Larry so bad that his arm came about to the left and doused Raedene with gas—which immediately ignited. The three of us were on top of her, burning along with her. It's virtually impossible to put out a gas fire with your hands and body. Mom came out of the house and tore off Raedene's burning clothes. She was screaming in terrible pain. Her face and arms and legs received third-degree burns. For the next two weeks, I helped Mom out, taking turns sitting with Raedene in the hospital, in Temple, TX. Her scars are visible to this day and she is now sixty-two years old.

On my way back to Thomasville, I stopped by and visited Jackie and she still wouldn't agree to come with me.

While stationed at Thomasville AFS, Alabama, two of us from the Orderly Room volunteered to go flying with our Commander, Captain Craig, on a Sunday in 1959. We were to fly to Florida, pick up some chairs, and be back the same day. Not so, Capt. Craig drove us to Selma, Alabama, where we boarded a C-47, DC-3, from Craig AFB. First, we transported passengers to Sheppard AFB in Texas. Because of stormy weather, we could not leave Sheppard AFB. After a while, we were able to leave and fly to Reese AFB in Lubbock where we spent the night. The next day we flew to Hensley Field in Grand Prairie, Texas. I called my Holtman friends and we had beer together. The next day, Tuesday, we were allowed to fly to Cross City, Florida. During the trip, Capt. Craig let me pilot the plane while he went to the restroom. We picked up the chairs and flew back to Thomasville, arriving by bedtime. The three days in the same clothes, and no toothbrush was quite an experience.

Again, in 1960, three of us from the Orderly Room, including First Sergeant, went flying with our Commander while stationed at Pagwa River AFS, Canada.

We were in a 5-seat L-20 aircraft, which is just a little bigger than a Piper Cub. We flew over the next Pine Tree Line Base in Manitoba, Canada. Our First Sergeant got air sick and threw up in a paper bag. On our return trip we saw several moose, and the beginning of a forest fire, which we reported to the Canadian authorities.

I can recall many incidents that occurred while I was stationed at Pagwa River, Ontario. We lived in three-person dorm rooms. One night, I awoke to hear splashing at the foot of my bed. A guy, drunk on beer, came into our room thinking it was the central latrine, did his business, peeing on the floor and on the end of my bed. I lead him down the hall to his room and went back to begin the nasty task of cleaning up. It took me an hour and I still couldn't get rid of the smell. After that, we locked our doors at night! Lucky for my roommates, they were gone for the evening.

During my tour in Canada, we fished a lot in the summer. There was an abundance of Northern Pike and Sturgeons. The cooks would fry the fish and serve them at each of the three bars on base: The Officer's Club, the NCO Club and the Airmen's Club. Beer and fish at 9:00 p.m. was really good. My fishing crew was the only ones bringing in enough fish for everyone. A favorite fishing lake was twenty miles away, accessible across Pagwa River by jeep. One day four of us from the Orderly Room, Personnel, got in the Jeep to go fishing. The driver could not see the shallow path in the river and we landed in deep water. We grabbed everything and placed it on top of the Jeep out of the water. I saw Sgt. Dunn's tackle box slide off the top of the Jeep into the water and go under. I dove under water and came up with the tackle box. I lost my sunglasses in the process. We were rescued by another Jeep and went on our fishing trip after we dried off.

Another fishing trip I recall was when Sgt. Tony, from Fon-du-lac, WI and I went by "put-put-car." The sectional railroad work crew, at Pagwa River

AFS, left every day to work on the bad parts of the railroad track. They had an extra trailer that we rode on. They let us off about ten miles from the base and agreed to pick us up at 4:00 p.m. on their way back home. The mosquitoes commanded half the air space. We had to wear mosquito nets over our heads and it was hot! We caught lots of trout in the live water over a beaver dam on a small lake. We had to wrap the slimy fish in my raincoat on our return trip on the put-put-car.

Since I'm on the subject of fishing, I may as well devote this chapter to that subject. I recall an incident while we were in high school. About four of us guys were in Marlin, our favorite hangout town probably because we loved dating the girls from Marlin, and also because the manager of one of the movie theaters let us football players in free of charge. 1 guess because we were a drawing card for more attendance. Anyway, it was a rainy day and the Marlin Lake spillway was overflowing with fish. We were dipping up fish everywhere with a net. We didn't know there was a city ordinance against it, and the city caretaker caught us, reprimanded us and told us to appear before the city judge the following Monday. It was only a scare tactic, but it worked. We appeared before the judge and got another lecture.

In my younger years, and even during high school, Dad taught me how to rock fish, noodling. In Texas, noodling for fish was illegal. I've asked and been forgiven for this sin. The reason is that catfish lay their eggs under rocks and if you capture the fish, then you have prevented the hatching of millions of fish. In the State of Oklahoma, noodling is legal. During my life, I have caught many pounds of fish by rock fishing. After a successful day of noodling, your hands and fingers will be raw from fish teeth marks.

One year, Dennis Morris and I backpacked up about a mile above the falls on the Brazos River. In one load, the two of us carried enough food, pots and pans, fishing gear, minnow seine, buckets, sleeping gear, and dry clothing for an overnight stay. We boiled the river water to drink and cook with. The return trip the next day was even heavier because we caught several pounds of fish.

On another occasion, I went with Mr. Morris and his sons, T.J. and Dennis. We trot-line fished above the gravel pits on the Brazos River, near Cedar Springs. The Morris' technique of fishing was different than I was accustomed to. We waded out in waist-deep water to set out several trot lines, baited them, and ran them every hour until 3:00 a.m. Then each one of them crawled into their cotton-picking sacks and went to sleep. I had no sack, so I covered myself with warm sand near the camp fire and slept that way. The next day we went home with about fifty fish.

Another fishing event occurred around 1973, while I was still in the Air Force, stationed at Randolph AFB in San Antonio. On a weekend, I went home and my brother John, my cousin Louis and I took John's boat and trot line fished in our old favorite *brush hole* on the Brazos River. We caught a good catch during the night, including a five-pound yellow cat (flat head). We put the fish in Dad's old, wire, mesh live box. The next morning, the five pounder and several others were gone. Evidence was, that a raccoon had broken into the box, and helped himself to our catch. Our fishing trip turned into a coon hunt!

When I was about eight years old, Dad and I, and Dad's old friend, Irvin Franz, from Rosebud, Texas, went fishing at the old brush hole, on the Brazos River, near Pool Creek. Irv always desired to have a bottle of whiskey when he went fishing. Dad liked whiskey too, but he didn't think that drinking and serious fishing went together. At home, Dad drank whiskey for medicine. In the old days Dad smoked and coughed a lot. He blamed his coughing on working in the cotton gin. Anyway, Dad and Irv were putting out trotlines from a boat. Dad was paddling the boat while Irv was unraveling the trotline. Irv stood up in the boat and, being tipsy from booze, he turned the boat over. Dad held onto the boat and retrieved the paddles and other fishing gear and pulled the boat to shallow water. Meanwhile, Irv was struggling in mid-stream and couldn't get anywhere. I was standing on the far bank and it looked like Irv was drowning. He went under water several times and came up choking. What really happened was that the trotline and hook had caught Irv in the back of his shirt, and he couldn't move until he ripped the hook from his shirt. Once he broke loose from the trotline, he freely swam to join Dad on the far river bank.

Earlier, I mentioned that the falls on the Brazos River was a favorite fishing place. An interesting thing about the falls was that it was about a six-foot drop over sand rock that was gradual over a ten-foot section. The county had poured a concrete slab, 200 feet above the falls for transportation purposes. The water coming over this slab created a falls in itself. Many people thought that this was the actual falls. The water above the falls was only about knee deep, but we trot-line fished this shallow water and caught many fish.

The following is an article from the Will Rogers United Methodist Church weekly paper with yet another fishing story:

"They called him, 'Sonny.' Born in a farm house in Westphalia, Texas, the year after Will Rogers died in a plane crash. This Texas farm boy grew up around this down-home ambience of a town the German immigrants named in honor of Westphalia Province in Germany. One of this town's claims to fame was *The Westphalia Waltz*, a song written by Cotton Collins, a fiddler with the Lone Star Playboys, who are perhaps best known as an early backup band for Hank Thompson. (If you want to know more about Westphalia, go to this website: http://www.texasescapes.com/ClayCoppedge/Westphalia-Waltz.htm). His paternal grandfather came from Sudetenland, Austria, now a part of the Czech Republic, and married a girl from Zurich, Switzerland. These Catholic folks saw their son marry a Lutheran girl, who was born in the USA. Sonny grow up in Falls County, Texas within six miles of the Brazos River, thriving on fish, crawfish, rabbits, squirrels, berries, grapes, and various other foods. Farm boys work from *see to, can't see* but always manage to find time to fish. Sonny was no exception. He can tell you many fishing stories. One time, his Dad and he were fishing on the Brazos, baiting a trot line. As he tells it, "We carried our minnows along with us in a bucket. We left the bucket on the shore after we finished the baiting. After dark, we returned to re-bait the hooks. Dad carried the minnow bucket and light and I reached in, caught the minnow and baited the hook. When we came to swifter water, I noticed a snake swimming between me and Dad—which was strange because one usually doesn't see snakes out in swift water. I reached into the bucket for another minnow and found instead, a snake in the bucket!" One can only imagine how quickly the trot-line was dropped and they made it to the river bank. It may be the first time he thought about walking on the water! They dumped the bucket out, they saw the water moccasin that was left in the bucket—probably the mate to the one that swam away.

I don't know if the preceding event had anything to do with it, but Sonny his heart to Jesus in 1951. He graduated from Lott High School in 1955 and went to work as a tile-setters helper. Soon, our friend joined the Air Force and served our country as a Personnel Superintendent. After the Air Force, he owned and operated a hotel gift shop, a used book store, and worked as a truck driver, bus driver, rural mail carrier, and Manpower training director.

December 2, 1961, this man of many talents married his beautiful wife of forty-five years. They have four children and eight grandchildren, each of whom is greatly treasured. He finds his faith to be an essential part of his life and credits God for getting him where he is in life. Our friend praises God for allowing him to be an instrument of grace to his family and to those he meets in daily life. This has been an important focus for him, especially after 1989, when he was filled with the Holy Spirit. Gospel music is enjoyed by our friend. He and his wife sang a wonderful southern gospel song, "Suppertime," together at his mother's funeral. With appropriate humbleness, our friend Garland Pelzel, understands the truth of his favorite scripture, John 15:5, which says, "Yes, I am the vine; you are the branches. Those who remain in Me and I in them, will produce much fruit. For apart from Me, you can do nothing." Garland, his wife Sue, are grateful that God's grace has produced much fruit through them. And we say "Thanks for being in our church family!"'

In July 1959, I received orders for a September assignment to Pagwa River AFS, Canada. At the same time, I received word from Jackie that she was ready to join me in Alabama. I found a house to rent and went back to Houma. I did not tell her that I had received orders for a remote assignment when I brought her back. I had it set up with the Air

Policeman at the gate to tell us this news when I got her to Thomasville.

Those two months away from her parents were delightful. Thomasville was a small town with less than 2,000 people and everyone knew each other. We joined The First Baptist Church, went roller skating, went to the movies, and one weekend we went to Montgomery and visited some of her relatives. Jackie was born in Fairfax, Alabama. They opened a new swimming pool on base and we went often. Things were going so well, we decided to try and make her pregnant.

Reluctantly, we returned her to live with her parents again, while I was in Canada. I received news shortly thereafter that she was pregnant. I came home on another thirty-day leave for Christmas and she was already in maternity clothes. We got to spend more quality time together. We visited my folks, my sister Carol, and Billy Jim in San Antonio, and the Boettgers in Port Arthur.

The 1957 Chevy was not running very well during this time period and we didn't want to borrow money to have it fixed, so we agreed to let the finance company repossess it. A dumb decision! So, in early 1960, they repossessed it. Later we got a bill to pay 550 dollars. Why? After a car is repossessed, they auction off the car. If they don't make enough on the auction to pay what you owe, by law, you must pay the difference. The finance company doesn't lose. So, we continued to pay on a car we no longer owned.

In January 1960, I returned to Canada to finish off my tour. Clarice called me on May 6,

1960 and told me I was the father of a baby girl and we named her Deborah Kay Pelzel. I came home on Sept. 8, 1960 to see my daughter for the first time. After being home for one week with my wife and daughter, Jackie told me to pack up and leave. She didn't want us to be together anymore.

Reluctantly, I put all my belongings, except my high school ring, into this old 1954 Ford that Jackie acquired from a relative. She never did return my high school ring. I told her I was going out to the base to stay. Instead, I hit the road for Texas. I took the backroads in case they would send the police to stop me from leaving. I didn't have the title to the car, for one thing. My parents were disappointed because I came home without their new granddaughter. This really was a worrisome situation. I had received my second choice for my next base assignment, which was Ellington AFB, Houston, TX. Jackie had already shipped out household goods, clothing, baby stuff and furniture. It was in storage in Houston. We had ninety-days to retrieve it.

This was early fall 1960. It was cotton-picking time back home on the farm. I was bored. I reported to base and went about my life. Every week, Jackie would call my commander and demand that I return her and the baby's stuff. I left everything in storage until the last minute, still hoping she would join me in Houston. I was justified in telling my commander why I was not acting on Jackie's demands.

So, in November 1960, I rented a long trailer, picked up our stuff from storage and pulled it with that old Ford. It was a long 200 miles to Lott, TX, but I made it. My brothers helped me unload most of the furniture items at Grandma Boettger's house and storage shed. We put all of Jackie's stuff and the baby's things in the Ford.

Sunday, I made two attempts at leaving the farm and pulling the empty trailer behind. The clutch of the car was slipping, or it had too much spilled oil to make it work right. I was afraid to try it again, so I parked it and borrowed Dad's pick-up. I made it back to Houston and returned the rental trailer, then proceeded on to Port Arthur. On the outskirts of Port Arthur, I ran into a heavy pea soup fog. It was so thick, I got turned around on a butterfly exchange, going the wrong way. I hitchhiked to town and called Uncle Robert. It was 11:00 p.m. and he was already in bed. He got in his car, found me, and then still in the fog, we went to find the truck. When we found it, we popped the hood and immediately found the problem. It was the coil wire. We got it fixed and I went back to his house to spend the night.

On the next day, Monday, I visited with Uncle Walter, and went on to Houma. I unloaded all of Jackie's things, including the crib and baby things. I talked to Jackie and her Dad, held the baby for the last time, and hit the road again back to the farm to return Dad's pick-up. Mom and Dad didn't know I was back until they saw the pick-up parked in the garage. So, at noon on Tuesday, Mom drove me to Lott, and I hitchhiked back to Houston before dark.

Before Christmas of 1960, I bought an old '51 Chevy to get around in. From the barracks to the radar station at Ellington was about half a mile, but to the dining hall, it was over a mile, so transportation, even on base, was necessary. I got a part-time job as manager of the bowling alley on base. In early 1961, I hired a Houston lawyer to file divorce papers. Jackie wouldn't sign the papers, so we had more expense by having the sheriff's office in Houma serve the papers. I forged Jackie's signature on our income tax return check and used it to pay the lawyer for the divorce. Since being in the Air Force, I was domiciled in Falls County, so my divorce was through the County Clerk in Marlin, Texas. I had to pay the Houston lawyer travel expenses to and from Marlin. The court date was set for April 1, 1961. I was there, Jackie was not. The divorce was finalized on April 11, 1961. The dependent's allowance provided by the Air Force was

seventy-seven dollars and ten cents per month, so that amount was approved in the divorce decree for child support.

In Houston, I began to date again. However, I felt like my car was ugly, the old '51 Chevy, and I never had any money to do anything. It really didn't matter because in May 1961, I received reassignment orders to Oklahoma City AFS, near Tinker AFB. I picked up Mom, Raedene, and Larry and went to my sister Carol's house. Billy Jim sold me a 1959 Simca, a foreign car. Larry drove my old Chevy back to the farm and parked it. He wouldn't even drive it anymore. As it turned out, the Simca was *not* a step up. It was a lemon.

I packed all my personal belongings into the Simca and left Ft. Worth and headed toward my next base. I got as far as Gainesville, near the Texas/Oklahoma border, and the motor got hot and the power diminished. I made it to a filling station just outside of town. I caught a ride back into Gainesville and the gas station attendant was really helpful. He found a guy to go to get my car and pull it into town next to his filling station for safety. I had tools, so I broke the engine down and found that the head gasket was burned, allowing water to reach the pistons. I telephoned Oklahoma City AFS, and talked to the Officer of the Day, and got a verbal okay for a three-day extension of my leave. Then I hitchhiked back to Ft. Worth. The next day, Billy Jim took me to a parts store to buy a new head gasket. I hitchhiked back to Gainesville and worked on my car. I got it going and drove to Oklahoma City. I reported in at the gate and the security police said that I was AWOL because I was supposed to report a day earlier. I explained about the verbal approval of the extension by the O.D. They had a hard time finding him because by then he was off duty and they couldn't find the previous day's recorded notes.

At Oklahoma City AFS, we began our first CBPO—Consolidated Base Personnel Office. We started IBM Mechanical punch card records and reporting. We covered bases in Oklahoma, Texas, New Mexico, and Arkansas.

G. P. S. FOR LIVING

In late May 1961, I got in my Simca and headed toward Tulsa to attend my cousin's high school graduation. On the way, the head gasket began to malfunction by allowing water into the pistons. I made it to Skelly Stadium where the 643 seniors in the class of 1961 graduated. My cousin, Martha Ann Boettger, was surprised to see me. I spent the night with them and the next day Martha Ann took me to a parts dealer in town. I bought a new head gasket and again worked on my car. I returned to base on Saturday night. On June 1, 1961, I was promoted to SSgt. (E-5). On July fourth weekend, I took one of the guys to Arkansas to retrieve some of his personal belongings at the University of Arkansas. We spent the night in his old fraternity house. On the way back, we stopped briefly at Martha Ann's. I made a deal with her that I would return to Tulsa the following week with a date for her if she would get a date for me.

So, on July 7, 1961, on Friday, David Tice and I came to Tulsa, and I met a 1961 Will Rogers High School graduate named Sue Carolyn Looper. Never in my wildest dreams did I think that this would be the love of my life, my wife, the mother of our four children, and grandmother of our eight grandchildren!

The four of us went to a movie and then to an Irish pub for a late-night drink and a snack.

On Saturday, I did not have a date, but the Case family took us swimming and to an Indian Pow Wow in Pawnee, OK. On Sunday, Ann and David and Sue and I, plus the Case family, went swimming and picnicking on the Illinois River close to Tahlequah.

Both nights, David and I slept on Army cots in the Case family's living room.

The following weekend we returned. On Saturday morning, I picked up Sue and met her mother, and the four of us headed to Wilburton, along with the Case family. We dropped Sue off in Muskogee to attend a Rainbow Girls State Assembly Conference, of which she was an officer. We all went on to Wilburton Park Lake. The Cases set up a tent and Roy Case fished. That afternoon, I returned to Muskogee in the Simca and picked up Sue after her meeting. She was waiting for me, as they had finished early. We had a nice loveable ride back to Wilburton. About dark, it started raining. After we decided that the one tent wouldn't be sufficient, we broke camp, and all headed back to Tulsa in the heavy rainstorm. Once again, David and I slept on cots and Sue slept with Martha Ann. The next day, while the Case's went to church, I cleaned out the muddy tent and Sue fried chicken for lunch. That afternoon, the four of us lay on the living room floor and talked. I revealed to Sue about my failed marriage and baby daughter. That didn't seem to alter her feeling for me, PTL!

Sue and I set up a middle of the week, charcoaled burger cookout for me to meet her Dad and the rest of the family. David wanted to come and be a guest, but his relationship with my cousin was getting too serious, and he was already married, to a Mexican woman from New Mexico where he had formerly been assigned, and they also had a baby daughter. I discouraged any further relationship and refused to be a part of any continuing affairs. When I showed up at the mid-week cookout without David, Martha Ann was devastated. And when she found out the reason why David hadn't come, her feelings toward me changed. She was angry with me and she never has forgiven me to this day, many years later. I, on the other hand, am eternally grateful for her introducing me to Sue.

From that time on, I went to Tulsa nearly every weekend. I was sleeping on a very uncomfortable couch in the Looper's living room. It wasn't long before I met Betty and Joe Wisdom, who were very close friends of the Loopers, and happened to live just down the street. They had a spare bed in their son's, W.E. or William Earl, room and invited me to sleep down there whenever I was in town. The Wisdoms liked to sleep in on the weekend. So, I would get up at my usual time, between 6 and 7 a.m., and make coffee. Then I would quietly leave and go down to Sue's house, where she was always waiting for me. This arrangement continued until we got married.

One weekend I went home to Texas to celebrate Grandma Pelzel's eighty-fourth birthday, which was August 17, 1961. On the long ride back to the base, I decided that I wanted to marry Sue. During that week, I borrowed the money from Tinker AFB Credit Union, and bought a set of rings from the BX.

The following weekend, I got in the Simca after work on Friday and headed to Tulsa. The car conked out, head gasket, at the Chandler exit on the Turner turnpike. A woman picked me up, since I was in my uniform, and took me all the way to Sue's house—probably because I told her I planned to propose that night. That evening we were in the kitchen and Sue was on the phone with a friend.

While she was talking, I was holding her hand and sliding her class ring off and on her finger. At one point, I quickly slid her class ring off and replaced it with the engagement ring. Then I let go of her hand and walked into the other room, while she continued her conversation. A couple of minutes later, I heard her shriek and then laugh with joy as she discovered the new ring on her finger. And that's how we became engaged.

The next day, Sue took me to the downtown parts store to get the new head gasket and then dropped me off on Skelly Drive. A guy picked me up and said he was going to Oklahoma City, but first had to make a stop at an oilfield equipment company in Crystal City, which was in West Tulsa. I helped load some electric motors into his pick-up. He handed me one that particularly heavy and the weight of it pulled me down so quickly that it pulled a vertebra out of place in my back. It was very painful, but I bore the pain and went on and got my car fixed. That afternoon, Sue and I went to visit her friend Kathi Homan and family at their house. I asked her mom, Mildred, if I could just stretch out on the floor to ease the back pain, which I did. On Monday, back at the base, I went to the doctor at Tinker AFB, but he said it was only a muscle spasm and gave me pain pills.

Because Sue and Kathi were *best friends*, I decided to set Kathi up with a friend of mine from the office, Joe Cooper. They hit it off and began to date regularly. It got a lot easier when Kathi moved to Oklahoma City, to attend OCU. As it happened, her sister Nancy and husband Bill lived within a block of OCU, Nancy had also attended there. Sue was enrolled at Tulsa Technical College, in Tulsa. But on many weekends, she would come to Oklahoma City and stay either with Kathi at the dorm or with Nancy and Bill. One night after the four of us had double-dated, Joe and I drove back to the base, all the way across Oklahoma City with no lights on the Simca! Talk about nerve racking! But we made it okay. The security police even let us on the base without any trouble.

The car situation was bad and getting worse. I took it to a dealer for repair, and they said the motor's piston wall was scarred and it needed a whole new motor. I asked them to put it back together as best they could. It still ran, but oil was escaping into the water tank.

Sue came from Tulsa, by bus, on a long weekend, and we drove to Ft.

Worth. We hoped to trade the car in on a better one, but we didn't have any buying power and we still owned 200 dollars to Billy Jim. So, Carol drove us to the farm in Lott so Sue could meet my family. Raedene was a first grader in school then. We found Grandma Boettger downtown, in Lott. After all, it was a Saturday night. Grandma was with Clarence and Nobia Tucker. Clarence owned Lott's barber shop. We went by Grandma's house and she gave us two homemade quilts. Then we went back to Carol's in Ft. Worth.

By now, we had to push the Simca to start it. We had to stop a few times on the way back to Oklahoma City and add another quart of oil. Sue had a choice about getting back to Tulsa: 1) Take the bus, slow, or 2) drive the Simca. She decided to drive. I advised her to stop at mid-way on the turnpike, kill the engine, and add a quart of oil. She did and had some guys at the filling station give her a push to start the car. She made it back okay and called me to let me know.

During this time, I was hitchhiking to and from Tulsa a lot. It was never a problem when I was in uniform. I remember one time when I was leaving Houma, Louisiana, on Highway 90. There were two hitchhikers already there, standing about 200 yards apart. I picked a spot right in between them and a guy picked me up almost immediately. PTL

In November 1961, I joined Will Rogers Methodist Church, because Sue and her family were members there. So, from 1950 to 1956, I was a Methodist. Then from 1956 to 1961 was a Baptist. Since 1961, my membership remains with Will Rogers United Methodist Church.

On Friday, December 1, 1961, Sue came to Oklahoma City. Our secret plan was to do all the preliminary paperwork and pre-marriage stuff that weekend, and she would return the next weekend and we would be married. I borrowed a car from a guy on base. We went to the

County Health Department to get our blood test. But instead of it taking three days, they told us it would be ready later that same day if we wanted to come back and get it. So, we did that, then went to the court house and got our marriage license, which cost five dollars. We thought about hiring a J.P. to marry us right then and there. But we didn't.

On Saturday morning, Dec. 2, we borrowed the car again and went to a used car dealer and bought a tan 1954 Ford and a "time" plan. They were happy to oblige since we were getting married. We found a little 2-room efficiency to rent, I think it was fifty dollars a month with the water paid. We went back to the base and talked to the chaplain, Lt. Col. Ben Jackson. He was reluctant to marry us at first, but Sue convinced him it would not be a problem with her parents. And I told him we would find a J.P. if he didn't agree to it. So, he married us that night in the chapel at Tinker AFB. Those attending were Kathi and her sister Nancy and husband Bill, Joe Mack Cooper, and another friend, Bill Nessler.

After the ceremony, we went to our cozy little apartment and drank cheap pink champagne out of paper cups. Then we drove down the street to a pay phone and called the Loopers to tell them the news. They were happy for us.

Sue was able to transfer from Tulsa Technical College to Oklahoma Business College, OK, Oklahoma City. After she finished the course, OBC hired her as an instructor.

We settled into marriage very quickly and were happy to be together. I remember two events that happened in our first weeks that we can laugh about today. One was when Sue made Corn Chowder which was so bad neither one of us could get it down. And two, she got *hooked* by a smooth-talking magazine salesman into long-term magazine subscriptions, which we could ill afford. My pay didn't increase because of our marriage, like it might have. The "dependent's quarter allowance" was already being paid to Jackie for child support. So, our budget was tight, to say the least. Most of the trips we made home to Tulsa on the weekends were paid by either Sue's parents or grandparents. PTL

Then and now, I've always enjoyed pulling tricks and surprises on people, especially my sweet wife, who falls for most of them. In high school, on a Halloween night, I found this dead cat in the road. Us guys could always pick the locks on our school to get in. With wire, I hung that dead cat just above the Superintendent's desk. Thirty-five years later, Supt. Evans confessed to me that he had a tattoo on his arm, and I confessed to him that I was the one who hung the dead cat over his desk.

Another prank was when I hooked up a smoke bomb to my brother John's old Ford. The car was a lemon but in those days nobody had the money to buy a really nice car. My two brothers, John and Larry, got into the car in the backyard. I ran around the house to observe the unfolding drama. The car was smoking as they got near the front of the house. John stopped the car, told Larry to get out, and they both jumped out, and started running. John was hollering, "It's gonna blow up!" I laughed then, and I laugh now as I recall the prank.

I remember another laughing moment in 1961 when Sue's parent's house still faced Archer Street. We were all sitting outside in the yard on the side that faced Joplin Street. Some of the Looper's friends drove up, stopped short of the driveway, and everyone jumped out, yelling and arms flailing. A bee had gotten in the car and they were reacting as though the car was about to explode! I believe that God's medicine for living is laughter. I love good jokes and funny situations.

In March of 1962, we sold the Simca for $100.00 and decided to take a honeymoon trip to New Orleans. We visited some friends of mine in Baton Rouge. While we were in New Orleans, we stayed in quarters at the Navy Base on Lake Pontchartrain. And we went to Mardi Gras. Afterward, we went through Houma and I got to see and hold my ten-month old baby daughter. Clarice was not at all hospitable to my wife, so we didn't stay very long. From there we went to Port Arthur to visit more of my relatives and then to Galveston. We went on to Lott and visited my folks again and loaded the car with more of my stuff. I took out the back seat and we got a couch in there. We had moved to an apartment on East Aeronica in Midwest City, which was a big of an improvement over the efficiency. We needed that couch and other furniture.

At this same time, Sue's parents were negotiating to buy a cabin on Grand Lake. We began to spend a lot of time up there helping them rebuild and remodel the cabin.

And then, guess what? Something else happened. Sue got pregnant. She had to quit her job at OBC. We moved again to a 3-bedroom house on East 18th Street. It was a big house and we were able to fix one of the bedrooms up as a nursery.

The old Ford began to burn a lot of oil, so I rented a block-in-tackle and took the motor out. It was my first stab at being an auto mechanic. With a lot of help, I got the job done. But not before Sue was hospitalized with Toxemia, she was gaining too much weight and retaining too much fluid. I had to borrow Joe Mac's car that he had recently bought.

We overcame these obstacles, along with a few others. The baby was born on Oct. 16, 1962, Penny Annette. She was a breech birth and Sue's labor was long and hard—13 hours. In addition, the world was in chaos. It was the time of the Cuban Missile Crisis. We witnessed hundreds of loaded aircraft departing from Tinker AFB, headed for Florida. The conflict was aborted when Premier Khruschev backed down. Sue's mom, Marie, sister Marti, and cousin Deeann all were there to help out with the baby. I spent a lot of extra hours at the base playing war games, preparing for the worst-case scenario.

When Penny was only a month old, we went to Tulsa for the weekend. Sunday night, we started back to Oklahoma City. One mile before reaching the first filling station on the turnpike, the manual transmission went out on the Ford. It was a cold windy night, but fortunately, a black couple stopped and took all of us to the filling station. We called Tulsa, and, within an hour, Sue's parents were there. And five minutes later, her grandparents showed up too.

I had to crawl under the car and disconnect the drive shaft and tie it off before we could tow it back to Tulsa. The transmission was locking the free wheeling. The next day, Idie and Gordon let us drive their car back to Tulsa. The following weekend, we returned to Tulsa and we found a used manual transmission. We got the car into the Looper's detached garage. Working alone, I pulled the old transmission, and put in the good one.

Then the challenges just kept coming! We got a shocking notice from the IRS telling us that we owed them money, because Jackie was claiming Debbie as a dependent. They said that if I could prove that I was providing more than 50% of Debbie's support, to come to their Baton Rouge office to do so.

I'm sure that I was providing more than 50% of her support, but I know that Jackie would come up with fraudulent documents that would seem in her favor. This really hurt because when I filed income taxes prior to April 15, 1962, we had to pay extra money because Sue asked me not to claim her because we got married late in the year, it was only fair for her parents to claim her. So, I find out nine years later that her folks did not claim Sue as a dependent either. So, now I'm providing child support, but can't claim her on my tax report.

Something good came in 1963, on December 1, I was promoted to TSgt (E- 6). We were getting more pay, but that wasn't nearly enough. Hard times still came.

In 1963, we borrowed money from Sue's grandparents and bought a two bedroom house at 314 Russell Drive in Midwest City. The city post office is at the end of this street. The following year, we had a bad hail storm and I did the new roof job using cedar wood shingles. My brother, John Allen, was living with us then. He came to Oklahoma City to receive training in the electronics field. It didn't work out, because he went back home and got his old job back with Wilsonarts. That same year, our Ford was totaled when a guy hit me in a turn in Guthrie, OK while on an all-night fishing trip. We had to phone a guy at the base to come get us. Sondra McMahan was visiting Sue at the time.

We found a used car dealer in Bethany, OK to sell us a 1959 Nash Rambler station wagon. In October 1964, our second daughter was born. The same doctor that delivered Penny also delivered Lisa Irene. Around Thanksgiving 1964, my sister Carol left her four kids with her husband in Ft. Worth and came to visit us. We took her with us to Sue's parents' cabin on Grand Lake. We saw a lot of deer, but I couldn't hit one with the British 303 rifle that I had. More trouble developed when we got in the car to leave. It wouldn't start. Jay Dudman was there and he pulled the distributor and said that it was the cam shaft. So, Daisy, Marie, Sue, Carol and our two daughters drove back to Tulsa, while Tib and Jay pulled me and our runless Rambler to

Tulsa. Idie and Gordon let us drive their Chevy for the next week.

I took some time off the following week to try and fix the car. I was going to work on it in Joe's garage because it was cold. I came down with a stomach virus that really gave me a lot of pain. I couldn't eat or drink, it hurt so badly, and I threw up everything that tried to enter my stomach. So, we hired Snuffey, the neighborhood shade tree mechanic to work on our car. At first, we purchased the wrong size cam and had to take it back for exchange. He got it running again
and I managed to make it through the week.

But it wasn't long after this that the cam broke again while we were driving on south east twenty-Ninth Street in Midwest City. We took it to a G.I. mechanic this time, and after a week, I took off of work at noon and went and helped him put the car back together again. I had to have the car to drive Marie back to Tulsa.

Sometime in late 1964, my older brother Dalton called me and said that our Dad was visiting them in Pocatello, Idaho, and that Dad would come by Oklahoma City and visit us too. He arrived by bus and had a guy call me from the bus station to pick him up. This was in the A.M. and he was very tired and went to bed for several hours after arriving. Grandma Boettger was also visiting us at the time.

The next day I took Dad to the bus station and he continued his journey back home. Dad was fifty-seven years old then. This was his first vacation trip ever. This was the only time in my life that Dad ever visited me.

In January and February 1965, I went to the NCO Academy at Hamilton AFB, California, which was near San Francisco. That was thirty days of harsh training. While there, one weekend, I took the bus to Modesto, CA where Tib's half-brother, Bobby Joe, and his family lived and his mother, Ruth, and stepfather, Herman Nelch, lived. While they were driving me around Modesto, Herman suggested that we drive by the cemetery because he wanted me to see the plots that he bought. Bobby Joe said "No, Garland don't want to see them." The Holy Spirit was telling us something because just one month later, Herman died.

In April 1965, I was beginning to process the paperwork for re-enlistment when division headquarters sent me a notice for reassignment to Malmstrom AFB, Montana. I talked it over with Sue and we agreed not to go to Montana but be discharged from active duty instead. We found a rental home in Tulsa on North Columbia. So, after nine and a half years of service, our HHG were shipped to Tulsa. Sue got a part-time job with Sears. I got on with a steel company, chipping weld flat from welded joints using an air hammer. The noise penetrated my brain and after one and a half days, I quit this job. Grandma Boettger came to help out with our two kids. I couldn't find work anyplace. On the first of May 1965, I sent Jackie $10.00 for child support. A few days later she called me on the phone, phone number was on the $10 check. She said that she was remarried, and her husband wanted to adopt Debbie. I stuttered about and finally said okay. I believe this decision was in the best interest of Debbie and her life.

Things really got worse. We moved out of the North Columbia house and moved in with the in-laws so that we wouldn't have a rent expense. We stored a lot of our stuff in their garage. I began to work with Tib in the cabinet-making business as a helper and driver, making fifty dollars a week in cash and drawing unemployment.

I wanted back in the Air Force. The policy is that after separation you cannot re-enter active duty until you've been out ninety-three days. Well, after ninety-three days I could only come back in as an E-4, not E-6. Good news, in September, President Lyndon Johnson went all out on the Vietnam war, and opened my career field to prior service people without a reduction in rank. I couldn't meet the physical requirements, until I lost 40 pounds of weight. I immediately dieted, and on September 13, 1965, I was back on active duty as a Technical Sergeant making more money than before because all the service people got a pay raise on September 1, 1965, and I was then getting full quarters allowance for Sue and the two girls, as none went to Debbie's support.

We were based at McConnell AFB, Wichita, Kansas. I was put into Personnel assignments, a job I hated. I was in ADC Command, Air Defense Command, previously for nine and a half years. I was in the most chicken-shit command in all the Air

Force-SAC, Strategic Air Command. The Commander of SAC was General Curtis E. LeMay. The Chief of CBPO was a SOB major. My immediate boss was Major Ann H. Bonar, a woman who was very compassionate. Most of us workers conspired and the Chief of CBPO was fired but the pressure was still on because SAC came down with an unexpected ORI, Operations Readiness Inspection, and personnel failed. We all got extra work as a result of the failed ORI.

When we first got to Wichita, we lived in a rental house for a month then we found a cute older house on Greenwood Street. It was during this period that we decided to buy a new car and we could now afford it. We ordered it through GEX, a membership department store in Oklahoma City, that we were member of for years. In order to get the full trade-in value of the Rambler, I had to replace the manual transmission, and so I did. The new car was a 1966 Pontiac Tempest, metallic blue, air-conditioned, with automatic transmission. The list price was $2,900 and the financed price came to $3,200.

We visited my folks in Texas because they said that I needed to contact the Department of Human Relations in Belton, Texas. So, we did, and it was concerning the adoption of Debbie. I told them that I was living in Wichita, Kansas, so they transferred the case there. In Wichita, they had me counseled, and I signed the papers for the adoption to take place. In months that followed, I received papers stating that James Oates, Jackie's husband, had adopted my daughter who was not yet five years old.

One day, Sue needed the car to run an errand, so I came home at lunchtime and while she took care of the matter, I ate lunch with our two girls. Afterward, we swung on the front porch swing, awaiting Sue's return of the car. When she arrived, she got out of the car and walked in front of the car to the front porch. I immediately went behind the car to get in and told the girls to stay where they were. I started backing up and heard a thud and I quickly slammed the gear-shift to a forward movement, stopped, got out, and picked Lisa, 18 months, up off the ground behind the car. She was crying, and we couldn't tell if she was hurt or not. Sue drove me to work and took Lisa to the doctor's office. Lisa was alright. PTL

We had applied for base housing and in early 1966, we were approved and the government moved us in. We had a nice three-bedroom Capehart House, airconditioned, with a basement. Sue's folks visited us on base. We fixed a bed for them down in the basement. We put them on a mattress on top of wire springs. When they left, they forgot their dog Beejoe. I grabbed the dog and hopped into the car, parked under the turnpike overpass, jumped the fence with the dog, just in time for my in-laws to drive by, where they stopped to pick up their dog. They were really surprised.

In May 1966, I got out of bed and while I was putting on my pants, I felt a snap in my lower back and lightning, nerve, passed down my left leg to my toes. After that, I was in heavy pain and my left side was numb. I went to the doctors and they x-rayed and gave me some pain pills. I later found out that a vertebra in my lower back was broken and it permanently pinches the nerve in my back, called Spondylitis.

Our way of life improved, but my job was awful. While talking to Hqs SAC Personnel, I volunteered for SEA duty. They got me a December '66 assignment to Tan Son-Nhut AB, Saigon, South East Asia. This was about July 1966. My brothers, John and Larry, came to visit us. Sue was pregnant. The doctor told her to take it easy, stay off her feet, or she may lose the baby. While the four of us were playing cards, Sue didn't make it to the bathroom. She left a bloody trail—lost the baby. We were dumb and let her go most of the night in pain. At 3 a.m., I took her to the hospital and she was admitted. They put her on an I.V. because she was dehydrated. They kept her over until the next day. I went to Major Bonar, and she let me have an emergency leave. After Sue was released from the hospital, we went to the HCO Club that night and played Bingo.

At the end of July 1966, SAC Hqs called me and said that PACAF, Pacific Air Force, had an immediate open assignment to U-Tapao AB, Sattahip, Thailand, with an August 15, 1966 reporting. I volunteered, went to Tulsa, found a rental house, we, the family, painted it. The following week my orders were published, household goods were picked up, and we left Wichita. I got Sue and the girls settled in the Tulsa house and it was time for me to leave for Travis AFB, California. I went to the Tulsa Air National Guard Base and they flew me to Travis AFB.

When we left Travis AFB, it was by a C-141 Globe master with long rows of crowded seats. We landed on Wake Island for refueling, and then on to Clark AB, Angeles City, Philippines. We were there eight hours for repairs, and then we flew to Bangkok, Thailand. We spent the night in a hotel in Bangkok, and we walked

· around some. Then we were bused from Bangkok to U-Tapao AB, Sattahip, Thailand. The place was located a hundred miles south of Bangkok, on the southern tip of Thailand, with a port on the Gulf of Thailand. Thailand's economy consists of rice, rubber, teak wood, cattle, elephants, buffalo oxen, fish, cocoanuts, bananas, and Thai silk.

The purpose of our involvement against North Vietnam, was for South Vietnam, to help protect a sovereign, South Vietnam, non-combat country. In the late '50s and early '60s, the U.S. was afraid of the Domino Theory. If South Vietnam became Communist, so would all of Southeast Asia. These countries would fall like dominoes, one by one.

We got involved slowly at first in the early 60's. Our troops were sent in as advisors to the Republic of South Vietnam army, but things got worse. China and Russia aided the North. The U.S., plus some United Nations' troops, aided the South.

In 1965 and 1966, President Johnson ordered bombing of supply bases and fuel storage depots in NV, the DMZ, seventeenth parallel, Hanoi and especially the port city of Haiphong where Soviet ships were bringing in supplies. At the end of 1967, we had 500,000 troops in SV and 50,000 in Thailand among the seven bases. At U-Tapao we had B-52's to haul bombs, napalm, herbicide, Agent Orange, and other war materials. We also had KC-135's for refueling, and many other war planes. Additionally, we also flew missions from the Philippines, Guam, and Okinawa. By the end of 1967, we lost 1,833 airplanes and 1,204 helicopters. 767 had been shot down in North Vietnam. The situation got worse after 1967 and eventually in 1975 we gave up and pulled out. Even though I worked in Personnel, I was indirectly credited for involvement of the missions because I was part of our D.O.D. team. In working with the Air Force in Personnel, I was never in danger and was never involved with human suffering.

While in Thailand, I spent seven weekends in Bangkok. I had an Air Force friend who was a liaison in Bangkok, with a military vehicle and he lived in the Thai International Hotel. I lodged there also. Although we worked ten hours a day, seven days a week, we still had plenty off-duty time to eat and shop in town. I became very fond of fried rice with chicken and fried noodles with chicken with a hot pepper sauce on the side. Each dish was twenty-five cents.

I spent nine months at U-Tapao and they transferred me up northeast to Nakhon Phanom for the remaining three months of my one-year tour. NKP was right on the Mekong River next to Laos and only thirty miles across to North Vietnam. We could hear bombing every day.

While assigned to NKP, two of us from Personnel were selected to go to our satellite base at Muoknahon, Thailand, which was about seventy-five miles south. We were flown there with personnel records and forms, in a small piper cub plane.

Muoknahon was right on the edge of the Mekong River, and had no airport or runway. We came in, we banked, and turned halfway across the river, and started descending, and landed on a grassy baseball field. We did our job and the next day we flew back to NKP. Taking off from the baseball field was as exciting as landing.

While I was in Thailand, Sue got a job with Standard Plumbing and Heating on South Boston. She didn't profit much because she had to hire a babysitter for our two girls. We wrote each other often and made tape recordings. I mailed gift packages almost every month. The larger things I saved and shipped home when I left Thailand. The best buys came from the Philippines. I went TDY, temporary duty, there in April 1967 for four days. I tried to buy chinaware in Bangkok but failed. I wound up ordering it from Korea. I did buy Thai Lapidary Bronze Ware Utensils. I came home early in late July 1967, and Sue and the girls met me at Travis AFB. I could see them waiting through the fence. After one hour of waiting on the plane, marching to, and then clearing customs, I got to touch, hold, and kiss my three girls. What joy!

We tried to get lodging at Hamilton AFB but failed. We got a motel room instead. The next day we toured Golden Gate National Park and Fishermen's Wharf before driving to Modesto to Sue's grandmother, Ruth's, house where they stayed a month before I returned from Thailand.

A day or so later, we drove south and over to Las Vegas. We went out to Nellis AFB, but couldn't get lodging, so we got a motel in downtown Vegas, went swimming and saw the beautiful night lights.

The next day we went across Hoover Dam—what an awesome sight. Then we drove to Flagstaff and had lunch, sandwiches. We got to the Grand Canyon and saw some more of God's glory. We took a lot of pictures and the girls had us pulling our own hair by leaning over the edges, and not gripping the rails very well. We drove a lot that night and made it to Gallup, New Mexico by midnight. We found a cheap motel and within thirty seconds we were all asleep. The next day, we followed 1-40 to Oklahoma City. Tinker wouldn't give us lodging, so we got another cheap motel.

The next day, we had an appointment with Roger Bizzell, a realtor/broken that we dealt with previously. He showed us a lovely house in Del City and we agreed to buy it. If you haven't guessed it by now, my first-choice base was again Oklahoma City AFS, Oklahoma. We went out to the base to fill out finance papers to purchase the house and met my future boss and some that I already knew.

This was 1967, remember. I left OCAFS in 1965.

We arranged with the housing office to bring out our household goods that were there in storage. I also went by the shipping and receiving office and found my big box that I shipped from Thailand. The crate was too big, so I opened it in the parking lot and got it all in the car that way. For Sue and the kids, it was Christmas in July.

At first, we went to Tulsa and then on to the cabin on Grand Lake and fished, swam, ate, and ate some more. It was like another honeymoon, but just think—we were only married six years, and one was taken away.

Later, we went to my folks in Texas. My brother Larry and I went to many of the stock ponds in the area and shot frogs with 22-caliber rifles. I believe we killed about thirty frogs. They were good eating. Then Larry had gotten a small goat that they had a fit when I killed it to barbecue. They had gotten fond of this goat.

I constructed a concrete barbecue grill for my Dad. I had to haul sand from the river to mix the cement. I constructed forms from what Daddy had laying around the farm. It had a stovepipe chimney. Dad used this grill many times smoking catfish.

While I was in Thailand, and before Sue and the kids went to California, they went to see my folks in Texas and left this little miniature poodle with them. Upon homecoming, the dog wasn't very friendly and was full of burrs and stickers. No one wanted to hold or pet him in that condition. In 1968, we couldn't afford the high electric bills from the air conditioning in the house in Del City.

We sold the house and found a rental home, one and a half stories on Glendale in Midwest City near the flight path. Penny started in the first grade, in the Glendale Elementary School. One day I was pumping Lisa on my handlebars and pulling Penny by rope on her small straight-geared bike, meaning no brakes on that type starter bike. Everything was fine on level pavement and going uphill, but when we started downhill she came past us and I couldn't stop her. I threw in the rope and she crashed. Her face was beaten, and she had bruises everywhere. On Monday she didn't want to go to school looking like that, but she changed her mind and went back to school. After that, we got her a new bike with a braking system.

On the last day of June 1968 with Sue being pregnant and with the two girls at Grandma's in Tulsa, I convinced her all day that the baby was coming that day. The doctors said one more week. I was right. Michele Marie was born that day in the Tinker Hospital. Now we have one, two, three girls. What a wonderful delight.

In November 1968, I went, flew, to Keesler AFB, Biloxi, MS, for a short course in Personnel Management. On the way back, I rode part of the way with a SMSgt stationed at Sherman AFB, TX. He took me to Love Field, and I flew from there to Oklahoma City.

Then a guy wanted us to buy his house by making one back payment. We did and moved to a three-bedroom house on Stahl Drive, not far away.

SMSgt Shears had this 1955 Chevy Wagon that he let us buy for a hundred dollars because he was being reassigned. So now we had two cars.

During the winter term of 1968, I began taking my first college courses with the University of Oklahoma, Midwest City, TAFB Center. In the Air Force, we always got tuition assistance. My first six hours were in English and Government. Later on, in the spring term of 1970, I failed the course in Principles of Organization and Management. Upon opening night, this class had forty people.

The second night, the attendance was about twenty-five. Why? The professor's name was Amundo. A lot of people knew his style of teaching and dropped out. I didn't know. I stayed—didn't miss a class. I got an *F.* I learned nothing from him and deserved the *F.* If I went to his same class for forty semesters, I would still fail. He paced back and forth in the classroom as he talked. He called you by name to answer a question on a topic. If you couldn't answer, he would accuse you of not studying your lesson. Afterward, within two months, I took the end of course exam for Principles of Management through the USAF Institute and passed and was awarded three semester hours of college anyway.

In early 1969, we got notice that we had been approved for base housing on Tinker AFB. So now we were living on Chennault Drive right behind the base hospital. In addition to that, we got approved for a garden spot on Tinker AFB that was tilled and had running water. We planted a lot of stuff and it flourished. We had a lot of stuff to sell and give away.

Sometime in 1969, we got on a clacker-making binge. We made up a lot of them from rosin and glass molds, then we drilled a hole through them for the string. We took them to Ron and Marti in Burkburnett, TX, and tried to sell them at a garage sale. We demonstrated in a grocery store parking lot and sold a lot of them until the store manager asked us to leave.

It gets better. On June 1, 1969, I was promoted to MSGT, E-7. Our cars were paid for, we have money in the bank, so we bought a deep freeze from Sears. (The freezer is still good; we gave it to our son Troy in 2006).

Speaking of Troy, our one, two, three, yes fourth child was born on September 16, 1969, yes, at Tinker AFB Hospital, one block from where we were living at the time.

One week after Troy came home from the hospital, I had a vasectomy procedure. Since we got our son, we had no further plans for any more children.

DOD closed the Oklahoma City AFS at the end of 1969 and I was transferred to Tinker AFB under MAC, Military Airlift Command, headquartered at Wright Patterson AFB, Dayton, Ohio.

We began to have heater core problems with the Pontiac. While visiting in Texas, I chiseled the floorboard out on the passenger side to get to the heater core. We took it to a radiator shop in Temple, and they soldered it back together. When I re-installed the core, I forgot how to re-connect the heater system to make it work correctly. While in Texas, brother Dalton and his two children were there from New Orleans staying with our parents on the farm, so we, Sue and I and our four kids, stayed in Lott with Grandma Boettger. It was dumb, but we left the four kids with Grandma Boettger and joined Randall and Jimmie, Billy Kemp and Marilyn, Richard and Jeanine Taylor, Dean Powell and his wife, and John Allen and Barbara at a New Year's Eve dance in Zabcikville. The next day, Dalton hit a cow near Chilton which delayed their return to New Orleans. We ate dinner on the farm and got on the road back to our home in Oklahoma City. We met snow-covered cars coming from Oklahoma. By the time we got to the Oklahoma border, it was snowing hard. We could only travel forty miles an hour and the car was cold because of the heater mess-up. Troy was a baby of three months. It took us eight hours to get home. We normally made it in five hours.

The following week, we bought a 1969 Oldsmobile station wagon and sold the Classic Pontiac two weeks later. Then Ronnie and Marti had car problems.

Ronnie was at Sheppard AFB and they lived in Burkburnett. We brought them our 1955 Chevy Wagon and they later paid us one hundred dollars for it. One week after living with only one car, we found a 1965 Plymouth and bought it.

I got on this flea market binge. I would go to auctions and buy boxes of junk, then take it to the big flea markets at north east 10th Midwest Blvd. on weekends. Sometimes good, sometimes not so good.

In February, I attended CBPO Work Center Course, Phase II at Keesler AFB, MS. I drove or road-tested the Olds wagon. It was wonderful. On one weekend, I drove to New Orleans and visited Dalton and family. On Saturday, Dalton, his son Randy and I went fishing on a lake just halfway to Houma, LA. During my visit Lucille was justifying their move back to Pocatello, Idaho. A few months later, they announced divorce proceedings and Dalton's marriage to Daisy.

The work situation at Tinker AFB was great. I was in Special Actions Section of the CBPO. We processed separation procedures, promotions for both officers and airmen, retirements, awards, and decorations, officers' appointments in the regular Air Force, and flying status actions.

I wanted a pickup and this other guy wanted a car, so we made the even trade for the 1965 Plymouth and a 1963 Chevy pickup. I later bought a camper shell and put a mattress bed in it.

In early 1971, our world was crushed when my father-in-law, Tib, was diagnosed with cancer. They performed exploratory surgery but couldn't fix him. He smoked all of his life and he had cancer in his lungs, liver, lymph nodes and everywhere.

Ronnie was now a Sgt., E-4, in the Air Force at Sheppard AFB. He didn't like the military service. Now the opportunity was ripe for him to try for a hardship discharge. I helped him gather the needed paperwork and he got out of the Air Force as we left for reassignment to Randolph AFB.

I received notice for reassignment to Randolph AFB, San Antonio, TX with a June 1972 reporting date. So, we relocated to Randolph and rented a home in Schertz for a month and then moved onto the base. My initial work assignment was USAFMPC, USAF Military Personnel Center, but when they saw that I was fat as Santa Claus, they assigned me to the CBPO, Consolidated Base Personnel Office, and for a while, I worked Awards and Decorations, then I went to Records, then to Classification, then to Base Testing, and at the end of the year, I was in Career Counseling.

On July 30, 1971, just three months after Sue's dad was diagnosed with cancer, he died. In life, I only knew him for 10 special years. I took emergency leave, and the six of us traveled the long eight hours home to Tulsa. The funeral was Masonic, because Tib was a Mason for many years. I recall going to the Masonic picnic every year for the past 10 years. Troy Roden, a member of our church, and Tib were in Masons together. We have photos.

Life went on. The girls and Troy loved it, living on base at Randolph. They had choices of swimming pools, movie theaters, bike riding, and friends. It was a beautiful base and very secure. I often rode to work on my bicycle. We had a large two-story house with a fireplace and tons of pecans from all the trees.

Personnel, CBPO, was located in the Taj Mahal Headquarters Building. The flight line and NCO Club were one block away from the house.

Ron, Marti, and Marie visited us several times while we were at Randolph AFB in San Antonio. One time, Sue and I stayed awake all night awaiting their arrival. They had car problems in Dallas and had to wait for Federal Express to ship them the car part from Tulsa. While they visited one time, we all went to the San Antonio Zoo. While we were walking, we heard on the PA system that a little girl had lost her parents, and would they come to a central area to get her. Her name was Michele. We all stopped, looked around and our Michele was the lost little girl. She was four years old then. On another visit, Ron, Marti and Marie flew to San Antonio to visit us. We went on a shopping trip to Nuevo Laredo, Mexico. Marti bought a very long velvet picture in a frame. It wouldn't fit in any suitcase. They borrowed my overcoat, placed it inside and took it aboard the plane as a hanging garment.

Sue and I opened a bookstore in Universal City, just outside the main gate on Pat Booker Road. We named it "The Book Nook." It was bothersome. We received no profit the year we had it because we were always investing in stock. We sold it and got back all that we had invested in it. We took the money and bought a 1972 Chevy pickup with shell that was only a year old. We sold our old 1963 Chevy pickup.

Randolph AFB Recreation Center put out some of their surplus stock for sale by sealed bids. I bid on some guns and was high bidder on about ten. I wrote a check to pay for them but didn't have the money to cover them, so I went to the Vice President of Schertz State Bank and borrowed the money in about fifteen minutes. We used Schertz State Bank with the book store and had a good rapport with them. I sold every one of the guns for a profit. Later, I bought a brand-new Winchester Model 1400 MK II, N570253, 12-ga. 2¾ cham., from the Lott State

Bank for $110.00. Then I bought a 600 Jr. shot shell reloader and began reloading my own shotgun shells.

In September 1973, Sue and I, her mother, Ronnie and Marti, and Penny and Lisa went on a Mexico trip. Michele, Troy, and Chris stayed with a baby sitter. Chris was one, Troy was four, and Michele was five years old. We went to Monterrey and then on to Saltillo. Saltillo is where Brother Hugo Garza-Ortiz was raised. On the way back, we visited the Davis Caves.

After Christmas 1973, we returned from a vacation trip to Tulsa, an incident happened that crumbled any future that I had with the Air Force. Before Christmas, I had a discipline problem with a subordinate worker. I bent over backwards giving this guy plenty of time off, but he took more. He wouldn't come to work on time, so I reported him to the First Sergeant. They reprimanded him, but this placed him in need for retaliation, so this is what he did. He wrote an anonymous letter to the Commander indicating that I did not safeguard some test material, which was true, and this is the real reason. When test material becomes obsolete, you itemize the stuff on a destruction sheet that must be signed by the Test Control Officer, then take it to the base documents shredder. On the day before I went on Christmas leave, I had this box full of obsolete test material, all listed on the destruction sheet, and while I was shredding this material, the shredding machine broke. So, I took the remaining documents back to the office and locked them in the test room and went on leave. When I returned from leave, the test room was padlocked, and an investigation was conducted. The proper procedure on that day would be to prepare a new sheet on the material that was actually shredded, lock up the remaining material in a safe, to be destroyed at another time.

I was given an Article fifteen, under the Uniform Code of Conduct by the Wing Commander and was fined 200 dollars for mismanagement of my duties. I was assigned a new job in Career Control and Counseling until I was reassigned to Sheppard AFB, TX in June 1974.

I was still on the flea market binge and spent a lot of time trying to sell. We got a lot of furniture from a base auction at Kelly AFB. I wound up taking a lot of armed, upholstered chairs to my sister Carol and she kept and used them for years.

We made the move to Wichita Falls, TX and found a large furnished house to rent for a month and then moved into base housing. We were very close to everything we needed. I started back to night college on base.

Lisa and her girlfriend were interrogated by Alex, a special agent for the OSI, Office of Special Investigations. There was a fire in the garage parking area of the base housing next to where we lived. OSI had to find the source of the arson, because there were a lot of spent matches in the area. A nine-year-old autistic dependent boy of a neighbor friend was the culprit. Case closed.

In the fall of 1974, we made a trip to Six Flags over Texas. Making the trip were the six of us, Marti and Ronnie, and son Chris, and Grandma Marie. At one place in the park was a floating, hinged bridge over a pond of water. Troy stepped on the bridge and *splash*, his feet went out from under him and he was in the pond up to his neck. We witnessed the kid in the water, and it dawned on us that it was Troy. A young girl helped pull him out, although he was five years old, and could swim. We had no dry clothes with us, so I took him to the rest room, stripped him, squeezed out all the water I could and put his clothes back on, except we bought him a new dry t-shirt to wear.

I was still on the flea market binge. I bought old lawn mowers, restored them and sold them for a profit. A lot of time was spent on weekends at the Wichita Falls flea markets. I still own two different expensive antiques that I haven't sold in over fifty years. One is a twenty-one piece antique German-made Tool Collector's Cabinet Makers Set (see photo #10). The other is a ten-volume set of 1902 Eversley Edition of "The Works of Shakespeare". Sue and the kids went to Tulsa to visit early on a Thursday. On Friday, I hitchhiked to Tulsa and met up with them at Marti and Ron's house on Independence Place, right up to the door. It took three different rides.

In July 1975, I applied for retirement from the Air Force to be effective April 1, 1976. Since I was going to enter full-time college in January 1976, at Northeastern State University in Tahlequah, OK, while on terminal leave, my orders were published, and I got to move my family to Tulsa in August 1975, in time for the kids to begin school for the fall term. I stayed on base through December 1975, and commuted home to Tulsa on weekends, with groceries from the commissary. I also attended college at night.

I bought a foreign-made car from a girl in the Air Force. I drove it home one weekend to sell in Tulsa. I hitchhiked back to Sheppard AFB—no problem. We later sold the car for a profit.

When I left Sheppard AFB in late December 1975, for New Years' time off, I never went back. I was on terminal leave and began commuting from Tulsa to Tahlequah, sixty-two miles one way or one hour and fifteen minutes driving time.

In 1975, before we left Sheppard AFB, we acquired two white German Sheppard pups—a male that we named Apollo and a female we called Juno. Our new house had a six-foot high privacy fence around the back yard, which was able to contain the dogs, *except* when it thundered, or fireworks went off. When that happened, Juno would scale that fence like a mountain goat and fly to the front porch, which she scratched, and whined until we let her in the house. During the next three years, they produced several large litters of snow white pups, which we sold for fifty dollars each, and they sold as soon as we put the ad out every time.

One cold winter night, Juno gave birth to twelve puppies. We moved them out of the freezing dog house to a pallet in the garage, but she was having a hard time getting them dry and warm. So, I took six of them in a box and put them in the oven. When they were dry and warm, I took them back to Juno and took the other six and warmed them the same way. Once they were all back with mom, they snuggled close and began to nurse. And Juno was finally able to relax.

In March 1976, while on Spring Break, we as a family went to Denver, Colorado to visit Dalton and Daisy, as both had jobs there after Dalton retired from the Marine Corps, while stationed at the Navy base in New Orleans. Going to Denver, we had car problems near Burlington, which was about 163 miles yet to travel. It's a long story in itself. We were detained six long hours trying to figure out why this big brown Oldsmobile station wagon wouldn't run properly. A nice garage mechanic tried, impatiently, to solve the problem. He put in a new fuel pump and everything. Then we lost the gas cap road testing it. It took an hour to find it. We had a fourth of a tank of gas, but the high altitude wouldn't allow the fuel system to work. A full tank of gas solved the problem. Then we had a flat, and the mechanic fixed it for us. He only charged us thirteen dollars for a half day's work. PTL. Dalton and Daisy held up supper for six hours, until we arrived about 10:00 p.m.

All in all, we had a good time. We visited the Royal Gorge, saw NORAD in Cheyenne Mountain, Pikes Peak, the Air Force Academy, and Coors Brewery.

Troy was now playing t-ball and a lot of my time was devoted to taking him to practice and games.

During the summer break, August 1976, John and Barbara, their two kids Kim and Tammy, and Louis Zaleski visited us and the Adams, just Chris, one child, at the Grand Lake cabin. We caught some fish, but they really weren't biting that well. We had some good meals, although we were in financial need.

On April 1, 1976, while in college classrooms at the Northeastern State University in Tahlequah, I officially retired from active military service in the USAF. I went from tuition assistance and full Air Force pay to G.I. Education Bill pay and half military pay which is retirement pay.

During my twenty years and fifteen days service, I was authorized to wear twelve ribbons as explained as follows:

- A <u>Decoration</u> is a badge of honor of distinctive shape conferred upon a person for performing outstanding deeds, usually in service to his/her country.
- A <u>Medal</u> is a specific type of decoration. It is made of metal, usually in the shape of a coin, and embellished with an inscription, head, or other device.

Some service ribbons and service medals are decorations awarded to an individual for performing military service in a specific war, campaign, organization, or for honorable service, and do not necessarily honor the performance of outstanding deeds or military service by the recipient of the awarded ribbons or medals.

- One Air <u>Force Commendation Medal</u> (See Citation)
- Two <u>Meritorious Service Medals</u> (See Citations). On the ribbon of the MSM, an Oak Leaf Cluster signifies subsequent award.
- <u>Air Force Outstanding Unit Award</u> with one silver oak leaf cluster. The silver OLC signifies six awards of this ribbon: (1) Oklahoma City AF Station during Cuban Crisis, 20 Oct. 62 to 30 Nov 62; (2) Assigned Oklahoma City AFS 1963 to 1964; (3) Assigned U-Tapao AFLD, Thailand, 1966-1967; (4) Assigned Nakhon Phanom AB, Thailand, 1966-67 with V Device for Valor, courage, fearlessness, bravery especially in battle, in support of a war; (5) Randolph AFB, TX 1971- 74; and (6) Assignment at Sheppard AFB, TX from 1974-1976.
- <u>Good Conduct Medal (Army)</u> with two bronze loops (2 awards) for Air Force service from origin 1947 to 1963 when the Air Force got its own GCM.
- <u>Air Force Good Conduct Medal</u> with two bronze OLC (3 awards).
- <u>Vietnam Service Medal</u> with two bronze service stars: One BSS for Air Offensive Campaign, 29 June 66 to 8 Mar 67, and the other for Air Offensive Campaign Phase II, 9 Mar 67 to 31 Mar 68. These two offensives were: Increase air power and bombings in North Vietnam

including railroads, factories, power plants, bridges, river communications, fuel storage tanks and the destruction of Viet Cong controlled villages all over South Vietnam. I was indirectly credited for involvement of these missions because I was part of our DOD Team.

- <u>Republic of Vietnam Gallantry Cross</u> with Palm, issued by the President of South Vietnam because of our assistance to his country. Gallantry means courage, heroic, or nobility of behavior. The Cross is just the order of merit. The Palm (bronze-looking palm branch) means victory-triumph-joy.
- <u>Republic of Vietnam Campaign Medal</u> (1960-1975, total involvement).
- <u>Small Arms Expert Marksman Ribbon.</u> For expert qualification of M-16 rifle. AF never bears arms except Military Police and Pilots.

CITATION TO ACCOMPANY THE AWARD OF THE AIR FORCE COMMENDATION MEDAL

To

GARLAND R. PELZEL

Technical Sergeant Garland R. Pelzel: -distinguished himself by meritorious service as Airman Manning, and Assignments NCO, Consolidated Base Personnel Office, 635th combat Support Group, U-Tapao Airfield, Thailand from 16 August 1966 to 28 April 1967. During this period, Sargent Pelzel constructed Operation Instructions for Career Control, Assignment Section, necessary and vital to the activation of the GBPO. He initiated new duty assignments to numerous personnel that were 1 mal-assigned due to the geographically remote CBPO at Don Muang AB prior to relocation and activation at this station. He maintained current manning ledgers that were necessary to assign newly arrived personnel, and for the requesting of hundreds of manning assistance requests that sub sequentially provided vital and important in the initial build-up of this base. Through his outstanding professional skill and initiative, manning problems were alleviated within minimum time. The energetic application of his knowledge has played a significant role in contributing to the success of this CBPO and the United States Air force mission in Southeast Asia. The distinctive accomplishments of Sergeant Pelzel reflect credit upon himself and the United states Air Force.

- Air Force Non-commissioned Officer Academy Ribbon–For intense management training in January- March 1965 for overall Air Force Leadership
- Air Force Longevity Service Award with four bronze OLC, represents five awards, one for each four-year period of service.
- National Defense Service Medal for being a part of the DOD team.

In July 1976, Sue's step-grandfather, Gordon Montgomery, died. Her grandmother, ldie, had to be placed in a nursing home. On December 15, 1976, I completed all the requirements for a degree. So, at the age of forty, I received a Bachelor of Science degree in Business Administration conferred June 1977. The following is a recap of college semester hour credits: eighty-three SH in classrooms, nine SH resident correspondence, twenty-six SH authorized by the Community College of the Air Force, ten SH by USAF Institute and eight SH for General Military Service. During my career in the Air Force, I have received more than twenty-five diplomas and certificates for various educational achievements. In December 1976, I went to the Regional Office of the Veterans Administration in Muskogee and applied for disability compensation. On March 23, 1977, the VA approved ten percent disability compensation for Spondylolisthesis of LS on S-1. So, I began to get a small monthly check from the VA, however, this amount was deducted from my Air Force Retirement

Pay. The only positive side was that the VA pay was tax-exempt. In later years, I went to thirty percent but later it was dropped to twenty percent. I was now in a struggle to find gainful employment. Finally, in June 1977, I got this job with the Builders Association of Metro Tulsa, Inc., as apprentice Training Director. I recruited, screened, and selected applicants for training into jobs associated with the building constructions trades, acquired instructors, and monitored training programs, obtained jobs for students after initial training period, set up and monitored continued related training programs, disbursed funds and accounted for expenditures, maintained a close relationship with local government agencies such as the VA, Vo-Tech, State Employment offices, State Department of Labor, and State Accrediting agencies, conducted presentations to high schools and other groups pertaining to this government-funded training program, and supervised thirty-five trainees at one time during various levels of the training program.

In 1978, while I was working as a Manpower Coordinator with the Builders Association of Tulsa, I was given a paid meeting trip with my wife to Sarasota Florida. We enjoyed the fellowship, beautiful beaches, and of course, the food. Sue still says the beaches in Sarasota are the most beautiful she's seen anywhere in the world!

In May 1978, I became the Home Owners Warranty Administrator for the Builders Association. I managed the overall operations of the business which included recruiting, counseling, and screening of builders for membership, received, disbursed, and accounted for funds, monitored home enrollments and inspection requirements, handled complaints, conciliations, and arbitration actions involving quality of home construction, worked in close relationship with home builders, local housing inspectors, VA and FHA representatives, conducted presentations to various groups of people to educate them concerning benefits of the Home Owners Warranty ten-year Buyer Protection Plan, and supervised three employees.

In 1979, Sue went to Real Estate school, was licensed, and went to work for Century 21-Jim Kelley Realtors. I followed her that same year. I went to Real Estate school, passed the state exam, and was licensed, and also went to work for Century 21-Jim Kelley Realtors. Our jobs were to solicit listings and formulate transactions effecting sale of property which included selling, advertising, open houses, and referral actions, counseled prospective buyers and sellers on such matters as appraisals, market analysis, pricing, credit, qualifying, financing, net to sellers and buyers, and many other related functions, and maintain a good working relationship with various mortgage lenders, secondary loan companies and VA and FHA personnel.

Being in real estate at that time was not a good time to rely on this for a living. Interest rates were around twenty percent. You couldn't find a buyer to qualify at this rate. Our two oldest girls were in high school and our home debt was getting deeper with almost no money coming in. Bang! The devil kicks you while you are down. In 1980, Sue is hospitalized with Toxic Shock Syndrome. Later, the CDC, Center for Disease Control, in Atlanta diagnosed the cause of TSS was the use of Rely Tampons.

During our daughter Penny's senior year in high school in 1979-80, an event happened that would affect our family for many years to come. Penny and her friend double dated and ended up bar-hopping and having too much to drink.

Before the night was over, she and her date had sex which resulted in her becoming pregnant. It turned out to be a *one-night stand* and she never saw the man again. She was somewhat over weight at the time, so her pregnancy was not evident till after she graduated in May. While she was pregnant, she made the most difficult decision she would ever have to make—to give the baby up for adoption. On October 19, 1980, she gave birth to a beautiful dark-haired baby girl.

A private adoption had already been set up, with the adoptive parents agreeing to pay all hospital and legal fees associated with the birth and adoption. Because it was a private adoption, all records were sealed and neither Penny, nor the adoptive parents would know each other. Sue and I, Lisa, and Marti, Sue's sister, were the only ones who were there and saw the baby. Penny said she could not see her or she would never be able to give her up. It was a heart wrenching experience for all of us! But, that's NOT the end of the story.

I know for the most part that I have kept this book in chronological order, but because of the subject matter, I'll step forward to the present time.

In late August 2017, Sue decided to have her DNA tested at the urging of our kids and grandkids. She had always wondered about her Indian blood, since she and Marti had always been told their great-great grandmother was a full blood Cherokee Indian. So, going through Ancestry.com, she and Marti both had their DNA tested. As it turned out, they don't have any Native American blood at all—Zero, Zilch!

Three months later, in November 2017, Sue received a hit on her Ancestry account from a young woman by the name of Kathryn Hallquist. She said she was adopted and was looking for her birth family. Sue's named popped up as a possible one generation removed relative. And she said she was born on October 19, 1980 in Tulsa at St. John Hospital. Yes, she *was*, in fact, Penny's daughter. Thirty-seven years of prayers had been answered. More on this later.

Now, I'll explain my thirteen grandchildren. Some of them won't be seen by me until I reach my heavenly home that Jesus has gone on before us to prepare this place for us who believe. Two came from Penny, the girl from October 19, 1980, and Krysta Millennia Gabriel Crawley, born February 16, 2000; three boys from Lisa, Spencer Cameron Smith, born July 20, 1992, Tanner Ryan Smith, born April 20, 1994 and Brady Aaron Smith, born May 25, 1998, three from Michele, Jordan

Thomas Mullings, born January 31, 1990, Mason Ray Mullings, born November 4, 1992, and Kenslie Michele Mullings, born March 10, 1997, one boy from Troy, Dalton Blake Pelzel, born January 27, 1999, two from Debbie, an aborted baby in 1979, and Summer Rose Holder, born December 3, 1997, and two more boys from common-law, son-in-law John Collishaw, Thomas Collishaw, born May 27, 1994, and Matthew Collishaw, born December 22, 1998. That's thirteen.

Sue was healed and dropped out of real estate, and I followed her in 1981.

Sue went back to retailing with Gifts Ill. I helped her with incoming, freight, and pricing and I worked part-time as a distributor and inspector for Penny Power Distribution Services. Also, Sue's grandmother, ldie Montgomery, died on June 26, 1981.

On May 8, 1982, Penny and Richard Laws got married in our church, Will Rogers United Methodist Church, with Reverend Guy C. Ames, Jr. doing the ceremony.

Since flea market status was in my blood, I decided to open a thrift store. Found a location at 3204 East 15th Street. I found out real fast that it takes a lot of junk selling just to pay the overhead in a business like this. Since this didn't work out, I changed from thrift store to used books. I changed locations to 2122 South Memorial and rented space from the same investor, Buck Meyers. So now I was dealing in used books, and the name of the store was Bargain Books. It didn't take long to find out that no income was achieved at this business either. Troy and Michele were now in high school, Lisa was in college and Penny and Richard were struggling at different jobs.

In 1982, while Sue was managing Gifts Ill, she won a sales contest which was a vacation to Paradise Island in the Bahamas. It was a company trip and spouses were invited. While there, several of us rented mopeds to ride around the island. On the way out to the Bacardi Rum factory, I took a corner too fast and skidded in gravel. I tore up my knee pretty badly. People at the rum factory gave me first aid. I don't ride bikes anymore.

In 1985, I got on with the Post Office as a Rural Mail Carrier but after ninety days I was terminated because I was too slow. Frankly, I never worked so hard and fast in my life. The real problem was management. I filed an appeal and lost again.

Penny and Richard had moved to Dallas and were laying carpet there. They were having a rough time, too. Lisa had one of our credit cards in college. We maxed out on every card that we had because we were buying groceries by credit card. We had over 1,700 dollars per month in debt payments to make, and over that, we needed about 500 dollars a month in utilities, and about 300 dollars in groceries.

I again starting rebuilding lawn mowers and selling them for the money we needed. In 1986, I was working on a lawn mower I picked up for five dollars. I had it running with the top cover off that protects the fly wheel. I noticed the gas tank was leaking gas, so I got a rag to wipe it clean and it caught in the flywheel and pulled my left hand with it and chop, my two upper sections of the index finger were gone. I finished repairing it and sold it the next day.

Between the years 1980 and 1987, our finances were at rock bottom. We used a credit card to buy milk and bread. We maxed out our borrowing power. The real reason behind it all was *me*. I denied Jesus and so our heavenly Father denied me. I was so stupid to not understand this. We owed over 80,000 dollars and our monthly minimum payments were 1,700 dollars per month. We were paying nine and a half percent on a thirty-year mortgage, twelve point seven five percent on a second mortgage, eighteen percent on a credit union loan, ten percent on each of two car loans, ten percent on a business loan, four percent on an insurance loan, fourteen percent on MasterCard, seventeen and a half percent on Visa card, nineteen point eight percent on another MasterCard, and twenty-one percent on a Sears loan.

In 1987, we stepped into a real bargain with Embassy Gifts, located inside the Embassy Suites Hotel in Tulsa. We bought it from a lady who didn't know anything about running the business. Although we had to keep it open fourteen hours a day, seven days a week, we made it prosper. Of course, we had to borrow all the money to start with, but we eventually got it all paid back. Employee theft was a problem at first. Sue finally gave up her job with Gifts Ill and then it was only the two of us, plus a dear old retired lady named Hilga. We had the business six years.

A wedding took place on May 21, 1988, again at Will Rogers United Methodist Church between our daughter Lisa and Scott Smith, a sports loving guy who lived just a block from our house. Scott graduated from my alma mater, Northeastern State University, with a degree in Physical Education. Lisa graduated from OU, and then got her master's degree from the University of Tulsa as a Speech Pathologist. Reverend Larry Becker conducted the wedding. Later, Lisa, was hired on by Tulsa University as Communications Coordinator.

Scott Smith was born January 28, 1964, in Tulsa, Oklahoma. His mother, Ruby Jewel (Wooten) Smith was born February 6, 1933, in Subiaco, Arkansas. His father, Richard Lloyd Smith was born July 31, 1931, in Tulsa, Oklahoma. His brother Steven Lloyd Smith was born May 10, 1954, in Tulsa Oklahoma, and his other brother Richard Leon Smith was born August 30, 1952, in Tulsa, Oklahoma.

Prior to 1988, we were just church goers. We gave to the church but did not tithe. We were thousands of dollars in debt at the time, struggling to make double mortgage payments, credit cards maxed out, second daughter in college. Our monthly debt payments were more than 1,700 dollars, not counting food and utility bills. Satan was moving in on us, but something happened. The Holy Spirit moved in with us and we began to tithe. It was tough, but the money was always there. Things began to get better—as promised in Luke 5:38, "Give and it will be given unto you, good measure, pressed down, shaken together, running over it will be put into your lap." God often allows bad things to happen to us, so He can ultimately give us what is best for us.

While working at our gift shop in the hotel, I had lots of free time to read. I would rather skin a skunk than read, but every year from 1989 through May 1992, I read through the entire Bible. Since then, I have read it in its entirety two more times—that's six times. From now on, I'm going to concentrate more on the New Testament. Sometime in 1989, I was filled with the Holy Spirit of God. Not at once, but a gradual change came over my body. The Bible says that John the Baptist was born with the Spirit. All people now-a-days must first ask for forgiveness of all sins and accept Jesus Christ as their Lord and Savior before they will be filled with the Holy Spirit of God. Ask and it will be given to you, seek and you will find, knock and the door will be opened to you. For everyone who asks, receives, he who seeks finds, and to him who knocks, the door will be opened.

It's too bad and sad, that it took me fifty-three years to accept what God offers everyone. And the best part is that He promises eternal life with Him in the heavenly realm.

I was like the hard-headed Israelites who Moses led out of Egypt headed for the Promised Land filled with milk and honey. They disobeyed God, so He kept them wandering in the desert for forty years.

In the past, finances were the root of a lot of heartbreak hotels. It took me more than fifty-three years to locate the key to God's deposit box. Bring the whole tithe into the storehouse, that there may be food in my house. "Test me in this," says the Lord Almighty, "and see if I will not throw open the floodgates of heaven and pour out so much blessing that you will not have room enough for it." Tithing will shape the destiny of your life. It definitely has for me. All the money and everything is God's anyway.

In early 1989, I was prompted by the Holy Spirit to make contact with my daughter Debbie. Remember, she was adopted from me by Jackie's husband, James Oates, back in 1966. I went to the downtown Tulsa library and went through the telephone book looking for the Bergeron family. They weren't there. I was somewhat disappointed. However, just two weeks later, I was at home and the phone rang. This lady said, "You may not remember me, but you were once married to my mother." I shouted, "Debbie!" She couldn't get over that I was so elated to hear from her. I told her about my unsuccessful attempt to contact her. She was married to James Nichols and they lived in Picayune, Mississippi. Her grandmother had died, and everyone had moved from Houma except her Uncle Ronald.

Prior to this period, it seemed as though, we didn't have the money to make vacation trips except to fish on the lake. This year, 1989, Sue and I, Ron and Marti and their daughter Kim made a vacation trip to Picayune and Pensacola, Florida and New Orleans. So, 27 years had passed since I saw my other daughter Debbie. We met again and started a good relationship.

Debbie came to Tulsa for Michele and Kendall Mullings wedding on July 22, 1989, at Will Rogers UMC. The senior pastor, Larry Jacobson, was out of town, so the Associate Pastor Sonny Pleschke did the honors. In addition to Debbie being at the wedding, so was my mother, Irene, sister, Raedene, and Darral Hedges, and son, and daughters. My Uncle Walter and Aunt Ollie were there from Louisiana.

On Labor Day weekend, 1989, we provided the funds for Penny and her husband and Debbie and her husband to fly to Tulsa from Louisiana. All four of my daughters and their husbands camped out at our church's campgrounds on Ft. Gibson Lake.

Sue and I went on the road for Thanksgiving in November 1989. Penny wanted us to cook turkey and have Thanksgiving at her house in Pace, FL. So, we went on our way and visited Aunt Ollie and Uncle Walter on their farm near Slagle, LA. On the way through a logging town of Florien, LA, after dark, we got behind a logging truck going through town and when I thought I had a clearance to shoot ahead, a city cop got me for speeding and they confiscated my driver's license until the fine was paid. Then we noticed an oil leak while at their house. It was a busted power steering line. We got it repaired in Leesville, LA. We had a good visit. We had fried shrimp for one meal. We said goodbye and went on our way. Next stop was Picayune, MS at Debbie's house. We went out to eat and had some more seafood. We spent the night and the next day, we were back on the road again for Pace, FL. Sue fixed the turkey and dressing and we, the four of us, had a cozy Thanksgiving. After Thanksgiving, Sue and I and Penny went back to Picayune, 150 miles, and brought back Debbie with us, and we shopped at different places on the way back to Pace. After a couple more days, it was time to get Debbie back to Picayune and us on our way back to Tulsa.

Our first grandson, Jordan Thomas Mullings, was born on January 31, 1990.

This was on a Wednesday. I announced the birth on the PA during our regular WOW, Will Rogers on Wednesday meal. Church member Vadon Wyatt's birthday was that same day. Jordan had to stay in the hospital an extra week because of a blood count irregularity.

Sometime during the summer of 1990, the Hedges visited us, and we got access to our church cabin on Ft. Gibson Lake. We had borrowed our neighbors' fourteen-foot boat. We took the boat to the Illinois River near Tahlequah, Oklahoma. So, Darrel, Raedene, their son Dale and I went to the Illinois River, left the Hedges' van and went up river, thinking it was only about ten miles. The four of us floated all day. It got dark and we still never reached the Hedges van. We pulled ashore at a camp facility. The camp caretaker drove Darrel to where his van was parked, about half a mile further. The total float was twenty-two miles. Sue and Mom called Scott and Lisa and they also called the park rangers. We decided to leave the boat and my car and headed back to the church cabin. Scott found us as we were leaving. Quite an ordeal! The next day we went back to retrieve my car and the boat.

While on my annual October homecoming and dove hunting trip to Texas in 1990, Debbie and James came by the farm and the family got to visit with her. She was thirty years old at that time. Louis Zaleski was there along with Carol, John, Barbara, Raedene, Darral, and all three of Dad's dogs. It was a nice visit. During this same trip, I was called on to pioneer the thirty-fifth class reunion at homecoming. Everything went well. I still have the job as we continue to celebrate every five years.

During 1990, I had a routine doctor's appointment with J.D. McCarty located in the Physician's Building near Doctor's Hospital on South Harvard. Dr. McCarty examined me and then he said, "I'm admitting you to the hospital." I said what for, I'm not sick. He said that my blood sugar was extremely high. I argued with him and flat told him I was not going to the hospital. Besides, I needed to work and run the gift shop business located in the Embassy Suites Hotel. He gave this some thought and said, "OK, I'm sending you over to Doctor's Hospital for a shot of insulin and if this brings down your blood sugar count, I'll prescribe pills and you won't have to be hospitalized." It worked, but this changed my life completely. There are a lot of limitations being a Type II diabetic at age fifty-four.

On March 10, 1991, I was called upon to publicly give my testimony. This was on a Sunday night at Will Rogers UMC. The Senior Pastor was Larry Jacobson and the Associate Pastor was Terry Ewing.

Then, on October 12, 1991, I was called upon to give the thanks and blessings for our annual homecoming celebration for all ex-students of Lott High School, Lott, TX, my home town. Sue led the school in singing the National Anthem.

The next day, Sunday, October 13, 1991, the pastor of Lott United Methodist Church, Alan Wood, asked Sue and I to do the Laity Service. Sue led the singing as well as singing two solos, "Holy Ground," and "Victory in Jesus," and I read the Gospel reading, lead in praying, gave a testimonial message, and gave a short message on tithing.

On December 1, 1991, Sue and I were surprised with an anniversary party. Dan Anderson was president of our Sunday school class, The Faithbuilders. He called for a special Sunday school meeting for Saturday evening at 6:30 p.m. in Main Hall of our church. When we arrived, we saw our grandson Jordan playing in the Winston entrance of our church. As we entered Main Hall, there was Lisa, Michele, and Troy who shouted "Surprise" along with the entire Sunday school class. After we were there five minutes, I looked over the crowd and saw my mother and my sister and their family was there also. There was a wedding cake and a lot of decorations and they rushed us over to be seated while they showed a TV videotape. On the tape was Penny. She said that she was sorry she couldn't be there at the time, and wished us a happy anniversary, and then she said that she was going to do something about not being there at the time and Shazam, she appeared in person from behind a curtain. This whole party was planned earlier that year between Martha Foster, Marti, and our daughters. Lisa went to Charleston, South Carolina to visit Penny and Richard. They both flew home together, and Penny stayed and hid out. Raedene and family and my mother came a day earlier and stayed in a motel. It really was a big surprise. Also, a surprise, Lisa announced that she was pregnant.

Pastor Larry Jacobson had us repeat our wedding vows. It snowed that night, so early Sunday morning the Hedges and Mom got on the road home before the weather got worse. We went to Sunday school and church and afterward we helped Larry and Sara Jacobson have a parsonage open house. I remember our former pastor, Guy Ames, asking me if it was our twenty-ninth anniversary. Of course I told him it was our thirtieth. The day continued on because we went from the preacher's house back to church to prepare for our annual Hanging of the Greens program. After the program was a cookie reception. What fond memories.

A lot of important events are noted during the year 1992. I was elected President of Will Rogers United Methodist Men for a two-year term. As President, I initiated many fund-raising events, and we were able to donate

1,000 dollars each year to our church's building fund which helped jump start the building of the new Faith Center gym.

Two more grandsons were born in 1992. Spencer Cameron Smith was born on July 10, 1992 to Lisa and Scott Smith, their firstborn. On November 4, 1992, Mason Ray Millings was born to Michele and Kendall Mullings, their second child. I confess that I believe Mason has the characteristics and similar actions as yours truly. He's athletic. Loves girls and showmanship, and loves hot spicy foods, to name a few likenesses.

In May through July 1992, I initiated a challenge with our church that I could catch enough catfish to feed 200 people in our church. Sue and I arranged our gift shop work schedule so that I could go to the church cabin on Ft. Gibson Lake on Sunday afternoons, Wednesday afternoons, and Friday afternoons. I would catch, dress fish, and return home the next mornings. Each week, we would total up to the nearest pound, and show the congregation the results each week with a *news* ad in the church paper. On one Monday morning's catch in June 1992, a rainy, stormy night, I was able to add fifty pounds of filleted fish to the total, because I pulled in numerous fish and one was a twenty-seven pound flathead, yellow catfish (photos #6 & 7). These fish came off of two 300 foot trotlines and fifteen one-hook limb line, all done by wading in neck deep water. I had over 120 pounds of filleted catfish and the entire church loved it all. Reverend Larry Jacobson was pastor then. At that time, parties like this were accomplished in Main Hall of our church.

In February 1993, Sue and I both attended the Walk to Emmaus which is a three-day experience, which takes a New Testament look at Christianity as a lifestyle. It is a highly structured weekend, designed to strengthen and renew the faith of Christian people, and through them their families, congregations and the world in which they live. I experienced God's grace personally through the prayers and acts of service and love of a living support community. Emmaus lifts up a way for our grace-filled life to be lived and shared with others.

Also, in 1993, our contract lease with the Embassy Suites Hotel was not renewed and we had to vacate our gift shop space. We reduced the inventory as much as possible, sold some of the fixtures. We stored everything in our garage and initiated an agreement to open a new gift shop near the house at 2144 S. Memorial Drive in Tulsa. Our attempt at starting a new gift store in the Radisson Motel at the airport failed. So, Sue and I worked hard to open a Christian Gifts and Books store for the family and we named it Acts 2. After a few months, we came to the conclusion that it wouldn't work so we shut it down before going into more debt—a very wise decision.

That same year, 1993, I developed a problem with my neck, right arm, and hand. Sue and I went to Memphis, Tennessee to visit our daughter Penny and her Navy husband, at the time, Richard Laws. We went bowling at the Millington Naval Support Base. Afterward, my whole right shoulder began to hurt. I hardly slept that night and the problem still exists to this day. I made numerous trips to the Tinker AFB Hospital in Oklahoma City. They took x-rays and sent me through a CAT scan chamber and later they told me that they wouldn't do anything more for me and it was up to the Veterans Administration to take care of us. The final diagnosis was CT-Cervical Spine, neck, Pronounced Anterior bony bridging, spurring at C4-5, with compromise, intervertebral Foramen R (right) to C3-4, Cervical Stenosis C3-4. The VA sent me to Eastern Oklahoma Physical Rehabilitation Center. I went there weekly, until I found out that I wasn't improving, and that CHAMPUS only paid a portion of the bills. To this day, I cannot turn my neck without pain, my right arm hurts and my fingers on the right hand are semi-numb all the time.

On February 17, 1994, my dad died at age eighty-six. He had been in the nursing home in Rosebud, Texas, for many years. He didn't like it there and he said that he would escape. This is scriptural: In John 12:18, "Jesus said that when you were younger you dressed yourself and went where you wanted. But when you are old, you will stretch out your hands and someone else will dress you and lead you where you do not want to go." One time he got his suitcase or someone else's suitcase and left. The police looked for him for hours. His home was north of Rosebud. They found him on a gravel road a couple of miles from the nursing home, but he was found headed east. One day he was in his wheel chair headed out the front gate of the nursing home and all of a sudden, he disappeared. The attendants ran out looking for him and found him at the bottom of a deep ditch turned over in his wheel chair, laughing. So he really did leave the nursing home. He was taken by ambulance to King's Daughter Hospital in Temple where he died of heart failure. He now resides, body only, in Clover Hill Cemetery in Lott, Texas, in the family plot. (See photos #8 & #9).

On April 20, 1994, Lisa gave birth to her second son, Tanner Ryan Smith, in Tulsa Hillcrest Hospital. Penny came from Millington, Tennessee, to witness the birth of Tanner. When she returned home, her husband of twelve years said goodbye, for he had found a girl that he loved more. Richard was sterile, so there were no children involved.

In November 1994, I tested and received my CDL, commercial driver's license, in time to be hired by the Methodist Manor and drove the twenty-two passenger bus to Branson, Missouri. We took in eight shows and ate at some marvelous restaurants. In 1995, the Methodist Manor hired my wife Sue as their Activities Director. We both got to take the Manor residents to Branson and saw more shows. One was the Show Boat. I remember it being very cold and it snowed. The highways were treacherous. The weather was fine back in Tulsa.

During the time that we were planning for the Manor trip to Branson in late 1996, we both lost our jobs at the Manor. Sue's boss changed at the Manor and she, the head nurse, made things miserable for her and almost everyone she came in contact with. I personally asked the Administrator, Ed Hargrove, if he could do something about it. He didn't reply and just gave me a cold shoulder. Months later, while we were on the Kiamichi Drive fall trip, I told the Manor residents on the bus how miserable Sue was working for the Chief Nurse. In the next few days, I was fired by the Administrator for conspiring to manipulate the Manor residents to disfavor an executive decision. A few minutes later the Chief Nurse tried to chastise Sue by changing her job and holding her responsible for my actions. Sue said, "No thank you," and walked out.

So, now in late 1996, we were both unemployed and we were selling our house and buying the one next door. How could we do it? We continued to tithe, money came in from everywhere, our church family, and we sold a third car, left over escrow money, and briefly, unemployment checks. Then a door opened for Sue at Hillcrest Hospital and she began a job at the gift shop that paid more money than she ever made before.

Our old neighbors were trying to sell their old house next door to us on Memorial Drive. It was grown up and needed maintenance. After a year on the market, she was discouraged. She, in desperation, said, make me an offer. She was trying to get 79,000 dollars. Not real serious, I said, "how about 55,000 dollars?" She said okay, so we went from there. I began to clean it up and we made arrangements for our nephew to purchase our house at 2224 South Memorial. So, at closing time, on November 8, 1996, both of us unemployed, we bought the house at 2220 South Memorial and moved things across the fence. But, before we could close on the deal, the insurance company said it needed a new roof. In order to not halt the closing, we had to purchase the material and they gave us thirty days to install it. So, we did. We mortgaged a 35,000 dollar new loan for fifteen years at seven and a half percent interest.

After we moved in, I began to install the new roofing. After I had replaced approximately one hundred square feet, a young man drove up and asked me if I needed some help. I said, "No, thank you, I'll get it done eventually." He said that he was out of work and that he would do it cheap. I asked, how cheap, and he said five dollars a square. A square is one hundred square feet. I said yes. I believe the Lord sent His angels to help me. Psalm 1:6, "For the Lord watches over the way of the righteous." I paid him about 150 dollars so the complete cost of our new roof was 550 dollars. I contacted the former owner and her insurance company paid her 550 dollars and she gave me half of that. Praise God.

In January 1997, we started making monthly payments on the mortgage. Each month I paid in an extra one hundred dollars. My plan was to pay off the complete mortgage in ten years, instead of fifteen years. We actually paid it off in seven years and eleven months.

In the past, all of our automobiles were financed over a long period of time.

Since 1996, we have purchased five different cars, not new, but good ones, and we paid cash for each one of them. One was a Cadillac and one was a Lincoln Town Car.

On March 10, 1997, Kenslie Michele Mullings was born to Michele and Kendall, their third child, my granddaughter.

My daughter Debbie and Mike Holder were married on June 10, 1997.

Their daughter, Summer Rose, was born on December 3, 1997.

In 1997, I was called by god to serve as a member of our church's "Outreach to the World Committee." The committee oversees various VIM, Volunteer in Missions, projects in the states and Mexico and other parts of the world. As part of the team covenant, we attest that we are called by God to serve others in self-denial, through the power of the Holy Spirit. We commit ourselves to: love one another, forgive one another, be patient with one another, respect and encourage one another, work diligently and wholeheartedly, share Christ through our work and actions, and respect local tradition and culture. We further commit ourselves to the discipline of prayer, and an attitude of praise, and thanksgiving to God, that He might be glorified.

My first mission trip to Mexico was March 22-29, 1997. There were twenty-three people on this trip. We stayed in the First United Methodist Church in Mercedes, Texas. Our chief cook was Vickie McMahon. We built two houses in Nuevo Progresso, Tamaulipas, Mexico, and conducted Bible School there also. Our senior pastor Larry Jacobson was with us on this trip.

My second VIM trip was May 28-June 3, 1997, at the Boys Ranch, Gore, OK. A crew of eight people tore out an existing dorm room with a ceramic tile bath and made an office space and a dinette.

In July 1997, Vernon Upton, a Sunday school class member, asked me to drive a twelve-ton truck in the Upton Manufacturing business. I hauled steel and heat exchange louvers to various businesses in and around Tulsa. I stayed at this job until Vernon sold his company to a large company at the Port of Catoosa.

In October from the fourth through the eleventh 1997, I went on my third VIM trip. Twenty-three of us went to Rio Bravo, Tamaulipas, Mexico. We built two new houses and completed an unfinished third and conducted Bible training. Sue and Jim Ingold were our chefs. We stayed in the Rio Bravo UMC.

During August, September, and October 1997, I drew up my own plans and built a large hexagon-shaped gazebo in the back yard at 2220 South Memorial Drive. It had swing sets attached, an upper playroom, monkey bars, a sturdy center hexagon table, and benches to accommodate twenty or more people for games or picnicking. At that time, the cost of materials was under 1,700 dollars. We had a party in late October 1997, and Pastor Doug Burr dedicated the gazebo for Christian service. Later, I added a three-step waterfall pool.

Prior to 1995, Michael J. Pelzel, no relation, from Cincinnati, OH got our name from a public census report and began researching and collecting information about our ancestors. In 1995, he authored a two-volume book on Pelzl/Pelzel/Pelcl, past and present. Sue and I helped him collect information on our immediate Pelzel relations.

The book, published by Gateway Press, Inc., Baltimore, Maryland, is a two volume set, hardbound, with gold embossed cover and available in both an English language edition and a German language edition. Among the approximately 1,500 pages in each edition are hundreds of pages of birth, marriage, and death records obtained on microfilm by the author from the original parish registers, which are not located in the Czech Archives. Also included is vital data on more than 11,000 Pelzl/Pelzel descendants, plus their spouses. Many pages of personal recollections by contributors, who lived in the homeland of our ancestors, bring the history of the region alive. Following World War II, more than three million Sudeten Germans were expelled from the homeland where our families had lived, for up to 700 years. Stories of this expulsion are related through the eyes of those who were part of this tragic event in history. Reference the Weaver family page 28-36. Approximately 150 photographs of both people and places from the distant past are included throughout the book. Original birth, marriage, and death documents, most of which are written in Kurrentschrift, are included in their original form. In addition, each document has also been reproduced so they are readable by those who cannot read Kurrentschrift. Maps, historical background, and other items of particular interest to individual families, are also dispersed throughout the book. It is fully indexed. Michael and his wife Nancy came to Texas and we hosted a get-acquainted reception on April 11, 1996, at Westphalia Parish Hall in Westphalia, Texas. He personally signed my copy of his book. We had a fun time and ate Texas BBQ. Sue was asked to lead in singing, "The Star-Spangled Banner," and I was asked to pray.

Michael and Nancy Pelzel hosted a second Worldwide Pelzl/Pelzel/Pelcl Family Reunion on July 4-7, 1997, at the Regal Hotel in downtown Cincinnati. My sister, Raedene, and husband, Darral Hedges, drove up to Tulsa and the four of us went to Cincinnati. We got reservations to stay in guest housing at Wright Patterson AFB, Dayton, OH. On July fourth, we had an evening dinner cruise on the Ohio River and watched fireworks. The next night we had a banquet dinner in the Regal Hotel. All in all, it was a fun trip which included visiting the Air Force Museum at Wright-Patterson AFB.

On March 21-28, 1998, I went on my fourth VIM trip and with a group of twenty-nine people, we built three houses and conducted Bible training in Nuevo Progresso, Tamaulipas, Mexico. We stayed in the Mercedes, TX FUMC, and Regina Forrester was our chief chef.

On May 25, 1998, Lisa gave birth to her third son, Brady Aaron Smith. His dad, Scott, is training him to be an outstanding baseball player. His other two sons, Spencer and Tanner, are excelling in football. Their greatest cheerleader is Mom, Lisa.

From October 3-10, 1998, I was on my fifth VIM trip. Fourteen of us went and stayed in the house dormitory, located just south of Mercedes, TX. This house was donated to FUMC of Mercedes, Texas, by Truman Harkins' cousin. We built two houses in Rio Bravo, Tamaulipas, Mexico, and conducted Bible school. Ann Simpson and Truman Harkins were our cooks. Upon completion of this trip, Harold Shiew and Terry Davis got into loud and strong words concerning whether to take our accumulated garbage to the dump or to Mercedes FUMC. While they were arguing, I loaded all the bags into Harold Shiew's pickup and we, Harold and I, took them to Mercedes FUMC dumpsters. Harold didn't speak to me the whole two-mile trip.

In January 1999, on the twenty-seventh, Dalton Blake Pelzel was born to April Denise Anderson and Troy Scott Pelzel, our seventh grandchild.

In 1999, Sue and I were participants in our church's drama team. Dr. Mel Whittington, Associate Pastor, was our Director and play writer. Sue was Team Coordinator and I was the Stage Manager. The name of the play was, "Singing with the Saints." We had two public performances, Friday night, February 26 and Saturday night, February 27.

From March 20-17, 1999, I was part of the forty-three people who went on the VIM trip. This was my sixth trip. We built two houses and conducted Bible training in Rio Bravo, Tamaulipas, Mexico, and we stayed in the Weslaco FUMC. Vickie McMahon was our cook.

In September 1999, Sue and I, and Ronnie and Marti traveled to Northwest states and provinces in our Lincoln Continental. We left early on a Friday afternoon, hoping to spend the night on Offutt AFB in Omaha, Nebraska. No vacancies was the case and we kept driving. We drove until 3:00 a.m. and stopped. We found a place off the road in Marshall, Minnesota. Many times along the way, we thought about stopping at Wal-Mart and buying sleeping bags and bunking down in a sunflower farm. We visited Minot, North Dakota, Manitoba, Saskatchewan, South Dakota, Mt. Rushmore, The Corn Palace, and Walls Drug Store in South Dakota, and many other places. We blew a tire north of Rapid City and spent time at a SAM's Club replacing all four tires. While at SAM's, we first saw the large heavy-duty dining chairs that we now enjoy.

I went on my seventh missionary trip from October 2-9, 1999. Nineteen of us went and built two houses in Rio Bravo, Tamaulipas, Mexico, and did Bible training for the young and hungry Mexican kids. Again, we stayed in the FUMC of Weslaco, Texas. Virgie Boyd and Ann Simpson did the cooking.

God's grace proved sufficient as we had nothing to be concerned about as we approached the year 2000, Y2K. As we came into this year, we were perplexed as to what could happen. News people were concerned that the computer problems could not be corrected in time to make all the changes. But God was here as He always is, and everything went well. We still have our stocked supply of food and water.

In early January 2000, we received a bulletin from my niece Karol Kyno from Houston that she was to debut as an evangelist Saturday night, January 22 in a Houston Hotel. We just bought a Lincoln Town Car and I wanted to try it out.

On Friday, January 21, 2000, I traveled to Lott to spend the night and found out that my sister, Raedene, and her husband, Darral, wanted to go to Houston with me. My Mom was in the King's Daughter Hospital in Temple, so we visited with her and then went out to eat at the Golden Corral near the hospital. The next day, we drove to Cypress, a Houston suburb where Trevor and my niece, Kim Smith, lived and visited and had lunch with them before trying to find Karol. We left early, and it was a good thing because we really had a hard time finding the place Karol was preaching at. We got there in time for the program to begin, and Karol and Robert were surprised to see us. She did well in her debut. It took us three hours to get back to Lott and to bed. I got up Sunday morning and hit the road for home.

This email arrived on January 28, 2000,

"Praise God for family that loves the Lord!!!! I was so excited about Garland, Raedene, and Darral being there. It was by far the best blessing I could have received that night other than the fact God was there. For the past year and a half, I assisted a woman, three years younger than me. Gave and gave. She reminded me so much of me, her look, long hair, mannerisms, etc. Lots of fellow believers would say we

were alike. Anyway, she was an example for me, and I have had a burning desire to be this kind of woman for God. God has made a way, and Saturday night I lived a dream come true ever since I made a decision eleven years ago to give up my life and start a more serious adult life for God. Of course, I have to have a strong testimony, and with lots of trials and tribulations, I find more peace, joy, and happiness serving only God, Amen!!! My son knows more about the things of God at age six, than most adults. He has had Jewish and Christian left and right. He will tell you he's Jewish, but loves Jesus, Amen. And he was very excited about his mother's first meeting. He wanted to help and help. Yet he has let me know he's not too sure about his Mom being a minister because it has added extra pressure on him. I told him he would have to be good even more so, because a lot of eyes would focus on his behavior. True? Anyway, I LOVE YOU MUCH–JESUS LOVES YOU TOO. Signed, Karol and Robert Kyno Ministries."

On January 27, 2000, a huge sleet and snow storm came across the Southwest. In Tulsa we had twenty inches of snow. A few days prior, Mom was released from King's Daughter in Temple, and placed in the same nursing home as her sister-in-law, my Aunt Anne Fuchs. Mom died during the storm. Her pacemaker in her heart just quit. We could not leave Tulsa until Sunday, January 30, 2000, when the roads were safe. Her funeral was Monday, January 31, 2000, her great-grandson, Jordan Mullings' tenth birthday. Mom was eighty-four years old when she died. She and Dad had been married sixty-three years when he died. Raedene and I had talked many years before her death that it would be appropriate to have a grandson from each of Mom's six children to be pallbearers at her funeral. As it turned out, we could never locate Larry Roy Jr., and Troy was iced-in at Stigler, Oklahoma.

I wrote her eulogy with help from Raedene. Reverend Jerry Friedman, her pastor at Bethel Methodist Church in Robinson, Texas, told everyone that I wrote the eulogy and he didn't have to change any words. Sue and I furnished the song "Supper Time." We taped the song at home, then went behind the curtain at the funeral home while the music was played. It fooled everyone besides Raedene because we told her in advance. Interment was in the family plot of Clover Hill Cemetery, Lott, Texas.

Also, in September 2000, we four, Garland, Sue, Ronnie, and Marti, went on a vacation trip to New England. We spent the night in Lexington, Kentucky, with my cousin Donna. We took her to dinner and then she showed us the town. Of significance were all the ceramic, life-size horses everywhere. We went through the Pro Football Hall of Fame in Canton, Ohio. We had dinner at the Smugglers Wharf Restaurant in Erie, Pennsylvania, spent lots of time at Niagara Falls, went to a comedy dinner theater in Toronto, Ontario, Canada, through Montreal, Vermont's Morse Farm, covered bridges, a cemetery with unique headstones made from granite in Barre, Vermont, New Hampshire, Maine, Paul Revere Monument and Plymouth Rock in Massachusetts. We had lots of good seafood and took a boat ride to Martha's Vineyard. We also visited West Point, and the city of New York, the Chocolate World in Hershey, PA, as well as Gettysburg, and on back to Lexington, KY, and another night with Cousin Donna. On February 16, 2000, Krysta Millennia Gabriel Crawley was born to Penny and Glenn Crawley. Later, on June 3, 2000, Penny and Glenn were married at our home. We wanted the ceremony to take place under the gazebo, but it was raining outside. Dr. Mel Whittington from our church did the formalities of the wedding.

Glenn Lewis Crawley was born June 23, 1972, in Okmulgee, Oklahoma. His father, Glenn Crawley, Sr. was born October 20, 1940, in Okemah, Oklahoma. His mother, Naomi Ruth Turpin Crawley, was born August 9, 1942, in Fireball, California, and died March 21, 2007. His sister, Billie Robyn London, was born January 20, 1963 in Tulsa, Oklahoma and his sister, Leslie Nicole, was born December 2, 1963, in Tulsa, Oklahoma.

In June 2000, I participated in the *March for Jesus* parade in Tulsa. A Tulsa World photographer got a picture of me carrying a, "JESUS," sign and it was published in the newspaper (see photo #10). I'm so glad and happy that I am a Christian and I'm not ashamed to show it wherever I am. When we lived on Memorial, I had this sign attached to my garage door. It read, "JESUS IS LORD." One day in the year 2000, the following note was on my front door.

> "My name is Elsie and I'm from Kenya, Africa. This afternoon as I was walking around, I couldn't help it but notice the way you have proclaimed the name of our God at the front of your house. I was so touched that I felt like I would knock at the door and we share the love of God. I am saved, but I believe even non-believers who pass by your house know that you are saved and that you love God with all your heart. Thanks, Elsie."

I didn't realize it until I wrote this page, but for the last two years, Sue and I support a needy child by money donations through the organization called World Vision. The child we support is Penina Mbonani, from Kenya, Africa.

I am thankful that my life reflects God's goodness to others. Christians need Bible study, prayer, and fellowship with other Christians to mature. We learn Christ's ways as we read God's word, sense Christ's presence as we pray, and we are inspired to live for Christ as we spend time with others who live in the Spirit's power. The power is available when we tap into it. An example of this Godly love is expressed in this thank-you note from our friend Carl Cook dated sometime in 1999:

> "Dear Sue and Garland, I can never thank you enough for all you have done in blessing our lives and the lives of

others, as you have lived the Christian journey as few other I've known. You are the epitome of what *Christ in you* means. Thank you, dear ones, for all your prayer, support, and love and thank you for being there for us when we needed you. Also, thank you for the gorgeous gloxinia. I love it, just as I do my friends, Sue and Garland Pelzel. Sincerely, Carl Cook."

God wants us to find meaning in whatever situation we are involved with. In September 2001, He led Sue into directing our church's second drama play and led me into being the Stage Manager, again. Again, Dr. Mel Whittington wrote the play. This play was a sequel to "Singing with the Saints" and he named it "Everyone's Coming Home." Again, we did the play on two evenings. One on September eighth and another on September 9, 2001. Very successful and gratifying.

Pastor D. A. Bennett played the character that was a drunkard.

Also, in September 2001, the four of us, Garland, Sue, Ronnie and Marti, took a vacation trip out West. We were driving our green Cadillac. We go through Salina, Kansas, to Cheyenne Wyoming. We make it to Casper, Wyoming, by noon on a Sunday and find their First United Methodist Church and attended their service. Went on westward to Cody, Wyoming, where we are booked into a nice furnished motel home. Then on to Yellowstone National Park, Old

Faithful, and spend the night in Gardiner, Montana, where we saw wild elk in the streets. We took a sauna bath and had more good food. We went to East Glacier and spent the night and on through Glacier National Park, and into Alberta, Canada. Then we spent the night in Creston, British Columbia, Canada, then into Idaho, and Seattle, Washington. We spent lots of time in Seattle and Vancouver, BC. On our way to two nights of bed and breakfast in Portland, we got on the wrong ferry and spent most of the day on Friday Harbor, near Victoria, BC. After a visit in Portland, which included seeing the Spruce Goose airplane made out of wood by Howard Hughes in McMinnville, Oregon, we headed through Idaho and visited Twin Falls. The Snake River, where Evel Knievel made his unsuccessful attempt at crossing, was almost dry because of lack of rains during that time of year. We went on to Ogden, Utah, where Hill AFB let us have lodging. We spent a couple days visiting in Salt Lake City, which included listening to the Mormon Tabernacle Choir practice singing. One more stop before reaching home and that was Limon, Colorado.

In November 2001, I organized and emceed programming of a tribute to all veterans recognizing those deceased members of our church who were in the military. Stew and cornbread was the main dinner menu. Entertainment consisted of songs by the Joyful Spirits, Sue Pelzel, Sue Hershberger and Linda Paul, and a comedy was done by ventriloquist Joyce Lee. In memory of Sue's dad, Charles Danny

Looper, we used his Veterans Memorial Burial Flag centered high in the Faith Center.

On January 3, 2002, Sue's mom, Wanda Marie Warlick Looper, died while residing in the Oklahoma Methodist Manor. Senior Pastor D. A. Bennett and Associate Pastor, Dr. Mel Whittington, handled the funeral service. Mel read a memorial letter prepared by Marie's deaf granddaughter, Kimberly Stamper.

Interment was in Memorial Park Cemetery, next to her husband, Charles D. Looper, who died over 30 years earlier.

During February 2002, Sue and I, and Scott and Lisa, and their boys went to Florida and Disney World. We went in two cars and drove to Slidell, Louisiana the first day. We visited and had dinner with my daughter Debbie and my granddaughter Summer Rose and Debbie's half-brother, Michael Oates, who was studying to be a Baptist preacher.

It was a very long and tiring trip. We met and had dinner with Debbie's husband, Mike Holder. We spent two whole days at Disney World. Scott played golf one day, while the rest of us shopped. We all ate broiled lobster and fried oysters. The best!

The motel that we stayed in was in a south suburb called Kissimmee, Florida. The gift shop in this complex was orange-colored and orange-shaped. The last day there, we went to Cape Canaveral and Cocoa Beach. The morning we left Kissimmee, NASA launched a space craft. We saw it from our motel.

Again, it was a long drive back to Slidell. As before, we had dinner with Debbie and Summer Rose. On the day we lift Slidell, we got reports of snow storms in Oklahoma. We drove the scenic twenty-mile bridge across Lake Pontchartrain in New Orleans, traveled to Shreveport, and into Texas through Paris and got on the Indian Nation Turnpike at Hugo. From there to Tulsa was ice, snow, and slippery roads. Forty miles an hour was our speed. God protected us all the way. We give Him thanks and praise.

March 16th through the 23rd, 2002, I was one of the thirty-seven people from our church that went on the mission trip to Rio Bravo, Tamaulipas, Mexico. This was my eighth VIM trip. We stayed in the First Southern Baptist Church in Weslaco, Texas. Truman Harkins and I were the cooks, my first missionary chef assignment. Lots of early wake-up time and hard work, but very gratifying. I also drove my own Lincoln Town Car.

On September 9, 2002, Sue and I joined Troy at the Haskell County Courthouse in Stigler with his lawyer to obtain a divorce from Denise, and obtained child custody of son, Dalton Blake. The expenses were covered by Mom and Dad. We tagged along with Troy and a deputy from the Sheriff's Department when they took Dalton from his mother, Denise, at a house in Enterprise, Oklahoma.

On September 13, 2002, Sue and I and Marti and Ron departed from Tulsa in our Lincoln Town Car for a Michigan vacation. That night, Friday the thirteenth, we went as far as Ft. Leonard Wood, Missouri, where we spent the night on the Army base. The next day, we were going through St. Louis when we got a call from Michele, telling us that my brother

Dalton had died. That was shocking enough, but as we were crossing the Mississippi River into Illinois, my sister Carol called and told me that Dalton took his own life. He went outside at his home in Round rock, Texas, and stuck a 22 cal. Long pistol in his mouth and his spirit departed his body. As much as we know, he was always in pain, one hundred percent D.A.V., and the medication he was taking led him to this unacceptable action. He had a minor hand wound, Purple Heart, in the Korean War, suffered frost bitten feet as part of the Frozen Chosin in North Korea, and was driven over by a female Marine Corps recruit, who they were teaching to drive. He had pins in his hip and leg to hold him back together but was always in pain. He was a veteran of the Korean War and the Vietnam War with over twenty-three years of active service. He retired as a Chief Warren Officer-W-2.

In my own mind, I wrestled about stopping our planned vacation trip and flying to Austin for Dalton's funeral, but I could not justify this action. Dalton knew of our planned trip. We paid a lot of money in advance, we spent a lot of time calling and making reservations. The four of us were on our way in one car. He chose not to live, an ungodly ruling. So, I chose not to attend his funeral. The funeral was Tuesday, September 17, 2002 in Georgetown, Texas (see photo #13).

On Sunday, we toured Chicago, the pier, Sears Tower, etc. and spent that night at the Navy Lodging. Monday, we toured Milwaukee, and bought cheese in Wisconsin and on to our motel cottages in Mackinac City, Michigan. Tuesday, during the funeral, see photo #13, we were on a train ride in Ontario, Canada.

Other parts of our trip were Mackinac Island, Sault Ste. Marie locks, Battle Creek, Detroit, Springfield, Illinois, and Gateway Arch in St. Louis, Branson, and Silver Dollar City. Our car broke down in Branson, and we had to get Troy and Glenn to get Ronnie's truck and trailer to Branson and we towed it back to Tulsa.

From October 13 through 20, 2002, I was one of the eight people from our church that traveled to Rio Bravo, Tamaulipas, Mexico for my ninth VIM missionary trip. We stayed in the Methodist Church in Rio Bravo. I was the Chief Cook, although Truman Harkins started out helping me, but an emergency came up and he flew to Dallas.

On this trip we did not build houses, nor did we conduct Bible training.

Instead, we built and constructed fifty-foot long roof rafters to go over the second story of the new Hospital/Dormitory building in Rio Bravo.

During the first night, Truman and I saw a large rat in the kitchen. The next day we bought some large rat traps from the grocery store and set them out with peanut butter for bait. We also told Mario Santiago, the church custodian. He came up with a large homemade rat trap and we set it up in the kitchen. Then Mario warmed up a homemade tamale in the microwave and I ate it. It was probably the best tamale I ever ate. About 9 p.m., we left the kitchen to attend a planning meeting, and I turned the lights out upon leaving. One hour later, we returned to the kitchen, and sure enough, the big rat got caught. During the next day, Mario found his friend, Feliciano Lara, who had a .22 caliber rifle and they shot and killed the large rat. End of rat problem. In later years, I made my own similar type trap and have since caught dozens of squirrels and a raccoon.

From March 15th to the 22nd, 2003, forty-one of us took both new church buses to Rio Bravo, Tamaulipas, Mexico on my 10th VIM Mexico missions trip to build houses and conduct Bible training classes. Truman Harkins and I were the cooks. We stayed in the new First United Methodist Church in McAllen, Texas.

Sometime in early 2003, I carefully prepared documentation and sent in a request for re-evaluation of the mere twenty percent VA Disability I was receiving. They came back with a big list of doctor's appointments for me with local health care people including x-ray images of my back. In May 2003, the VA approved an increase to sixty percent. But since I was probably unemployable, sixty-seven years old, they approved me for one hundred percent disability. By law, they stopped my Air Force Retirement Pay and my VA salary was 1,000 dollars per month more than I made before. It gets even better. Under our great President, George W. Bush, effective January 1, 2004, legislation was approved to reinstate a portion of retirement pay. So, I am also receiving about two-thirds of my Air Force

Retirement Pay as well as the one hundred percent VA Disability Pay.

With the above income and my monthly social security pay that I started getting in 1998 at age sixty-two, our lifestyle allowed Sue to start putting forty percent of her income into her retirement account. And our savings accounts, and banking accounts are building, and we are surely not forgetting our God, who makes it possible. First fruits, tithe, are taken care of first as it is written in Exodus 23:19, "Bring the best of the first fruits of your soil to the house of the Lord your God." Prov. 3:9-10, "Honor the Lord with your wealth, with the first fruits of all your crops, then your barns will be filled to overflowing." Malachi 3:10, "Tithe and heaven will pour out so much blessing that you will not have room enough for it."

God graciously provides us with an abundance of monthly income. The umbrella doesn't stop there. Additionally, we have sufficient auto and home insurance, we each have good life insurance policies, and under investments we each have an IRA account and we share a living trust. I share all this to make a point. You can never out-give God!

Sue retired from Hillcrest Hospital Gifts in May 2005. She was already getting Social Security since January 2005. She transferred her IRA account with Edward Jones Investments. I also opened an IRA account with Edwards Jones Investments. We also opened a living trust savings account with Edward Jones Investments. In January 2008, Sue reached age sixty-five and is now dual insured like I am with Medicare and Tri-care for Life.

In October 2003, John Collishaw and his two boys Thomas and Matthew left New York and bought this large house in Broken Arrow, Oklahoma, located at 2312 West Vicksburg Street, Broken Arrow, Oklahoma 74012.

In January 2004, John and Michele got together and by June 2004 Michele left Kendall Mullings. Jordan stayed at home with Kendall. Mason and Kenslie moved in with John, Michele, Thomas, and Matthew. Later on, Mason moved out and joined Jordan to live with his Dad, Kendall. For tax purposes, all three of the Mullings children remained the responsibility of Kendall.

John James Collishaw was born December 5, 1963. His father was Leroy Collishaw born January 11, 1925, and his mother is Rita Reynalds Collishaw, born April 30, 1928. His father died August 7, 2002. They lived in Suffern and Pearl River, New York which is located near the New Jersey border, just south of West Point Army Military Academy.

John had seven brothers and sisters: Rich was born October 21, 1949, Cathy was born September 8, 1950, Janet was born October 2, 1951, and her children were Linnea born October 24, 1972, Jackie born August 26, 1982, Kristy born January 1, 1985, and John born September 1983. Brother Leroy Jr. was born November 29, 1952, and he died July 18, 2002. James, Jimmy was born January 31, 1955, and his children from two marriages were Sara born October 13, 1977, Amanda born January 9, 1989,

Jessica born March 20, 1992, and Melissa born November 3, 1993. Marion was born January 11, 1959, and sister Carol was born January 12, 1961. Her husband Joe was born September 6, 1961, and they have three children: Ashlei born October 23, 1988, Allison born May 25, 1991, and

Patrick born March 25, 1994.

John James Collishaw's first wife Maryann VanTassell was born January 30, 1964, and they had two children, Brandi born March 28, 1981, and Amber born February 7, 1983. John later married Rose Marie Muro, born December 20, 1958, and died November 29, 2002. She is the mother of Thomas born May 27, 1994, and Matthew born December 22, 1998.

From September thirteenth through the twenty-sixth, 2003, the four of us, Garland, Sue, Marti and Ronnie, went on a long vacation trip to New York City and Washington, D.C. areas. We left home on Friday after work and traveled to Brinkley, Arkansas where we spent the night. Saturday, we drove to Nashville, Tennessee, and ate lunch at the famous Loveless Cafe. We tried to locate the Pepper Patch Store but couldn't find it. We went on to Knoxville and spent the night with my old Air Force friend, Lowell, and his wife, Louise Cook. We had steak at a restaurant that had peanuts in the hull to eat and throw on the floor.

Sunday, we traveled through North Carolina and Virginia. We stayed at a Bed and Breakfast in West Point, Virginia. The next day we crossed the Chesapeake Bay Bridge, was closed two days later because of Hurricane Isabella. We had lunch in Dover, Delaware, at Shuckers Pier 13 Seafood Restaurant. I had fried oysters-they were terrible. It was raining when we got to Philadelphia and everything closed at 5 p.m. We got a motel in Mt. Laurel, New Jersey. The next day we got lodging at the Navy Lodge on Staten Island, New York. For several days we took the free Staten Island ferry to Manhattan, where we took the subway up town. If we would have driven, it would have taken hours. We toured New York City day and night, and always took the subway and ferry to our nice Navy lodge on Staten Island. Each time we took the ferry back and forth, we passed the Statue of Liberty. It reminded us of our freedom and of our ancestors who came from other countries. Reference our ancestors published in this book.

After Associate Pastor Joe Palm joined, or was hired by our church, he started this study series called Alpha Group. It was designed to have outside the church participants mixed with some of our church people to attend. Sue and I were some of the first participants mixed with some of the people from Meadowbrook Apartments on South Mingo. I was chosen to cook meals every week for this small group of people. Later, Jon Bartlett, from our church took over as leader and teacher. His mother said that he had entered seminary training later. We left New York City just after Hurricane Isabella hit. Baltimore was flooded. We couldn't get to the Phillips Harbor place Restaurant. There were a lot of power outages in D.C., and we stayed in Vinson Hall in Mclean, Virginia, outside of D.C. The first night there we had to use candles because the power was out. Daily, we would drive from Mclean to Falls Church, Virginia, where we parked the car and took the subway to the D.C. area. We visited all the places you could think of: Senator Jim lnhoff's office, the Capitol near the White House, the Smithsonian, Lincoln and Washington Memorials, Arlington National Cemetery, Vietnam Wall, and the Korean Memorial.

We made it to Lexington, Kentucky, to cousin Donna's house. We went out to a Kentucky horse farm and saw a lot of horses and a race track. We ate dinner at Lucie Meyer's Restaurant.

The next day we traveled to Ft. Leonard Wood Army Base in St. Roberts, Missouri. They lodged us in a three-bedroom furnished house for thirty-four dollars a night.

We went on to Branson, Missouri, and stayed in the Green Gable Inn while we attended John Hagee's Town Meeting with super stars.

In February 2004, we found this house that we lived in and enjoyed very much, 7487 East 20th street, about a half mile from our old residence. When we found it, it just got on the market that day. We signed a contract the next day and the owners accepted our offer a couple of days later.

While on my eleventh VIM Mexico mission trip, March twentieth through the twenty-seventh, 2004, I had to do some of the paperwork by phone, and mail, and fax. This mission trip was to Rio Bravo, Tamaulipas, Mexico. There were forty-two people on this trip and we gift two houses and conducted

Bible training for the kids. We stayed in the new Hospital/Dormitory that we helped build earlier. Truman Harkins and I were the cooks. Weather conditions during this trip were rain with a lot of high water. The buses got stuck at the construction site. The youth conducted Christian skits at night, in the park near the Methodist Church in Rio Bravo. Lora Thompson and Daniel Eisenberg interpreted in Spanish.

Upon my return from Mexico, we closed on our house and moved in. We got a fifteen year adjustable mortgage at 3.875% interest for four years and after that it could only go to 4%. We made seven payments plus $100 a month extra.

When we sold our old house on November 1, 2004, we paid off the mortgage completely. Then all we had to pay was our own insurance and taxes every year. Now we don't even do that. In 2006, the State of Oklahoma passed a *tax exempt* status for all one hundred percent disabled veterans, so now all we pay is home-owners insurance, PTL. From August 28th through September 6, 2004, we four, Garland, Sue, Ronnie and Marti, went on a seven-day Alaska Cruise aboard the Norwegian Star from the Norwegian Cruise Lines. We were booked on Northwest Airlines to Seattle and return, but when we got to Tulsa's airport on August 28th, our flight was cancelled, so they got us on a Delta flight to Denver and later on to Seattle. We spent that night in a Holiday Inn in Seattle and the next day we boarded the Norwegian Star and it sailed at 4:00 p.m. Monday, we cruised the Inside Passage outside of British Columbia to Alaska. We arrived in Juneau on Tuesday for shopping and shore excursions of Mendenhall Glacier and Salmon Bake. On Wednesday, we arrived at Skagway, Alaska, and our shore excursion was Yukon Territory Scenic Drive. Thursday, we cruised Glacier Bay, it was wet, sleet and snow, very cold and windy. Friday, we arrived in Ketchikan, Alaska for more shopping and our shore excursion was Heritage Town and Country tour.

Saturday, we arrived in Victoria, British Columbia, and our shore excursion was Butchart Gardens and Victoria City Tour. We arrived in Seattle early on Sunday for disembarking, went back to the airport, rented a car, and went to Pike Street Market near the cruise line shores and also went through the Seattle Aquarium. Then we went to the train station and boarded the Spirit of Washington for a dinner ride to a winery and return. At 1:00 a.m. Monday, we left Seattle via Northwest Airlines to Minneapolis and on back home to Tulsa.

In late September 2004, I was very unstable on my feet. I called Sue at work to come home and take me to the VA Clinic. The clinic took me into their walk-in emergency section and a nurse and doctor started checking me over. I could not urinate, so they placed a catheter in my penis. As the clock approached 4:30 p.m. closing time, the nurse said that I needed to go to the VA hospital in Muskogee. My wife, Sue, said that she could take me, so I got on my feet and was very nauseated and couldn't stand very long. My next choice was for an ambulance to come and take me to Hillcrest Hospital. I was in Hillcrest emergency for two hours when they finally admitted me. The next day, I was in x ray and in the kidney specialist department for a long time. Nephrology, Dr.

Thomas Kenkel said that my kidney function had deteriorated to almost seventy-five percent loss of effectiveness and could never heal. So now, no salt as well as no sugar or else. I stayed in the hospital four days and went home using a new kind of menu—no sodium.

In October 2004, Sue escorted our daughter Lisa to New York City for her fortieth birthday. They flew from Tulsa to LaGuardia Airport in Queens and stayed in a convenient hotel in Manhattan, close to everything. They went to a Broadway play and toured the Big Apple and reported that they had a wonderful time, Times Square. During the summer of 2005, our pastor Larry Jacobson asked that a group of father-sons get together and camp out on his property located in Coalgate County, near the town of Coalgate, Oklahoma. Some of us, including Pastor Larry, went there on Saturday before our campout to clean out trees and brush. My grandson Jordan Mullings, who was now age five, and I went early on Friday afternoon to do further clean-up jobs and fish. I taught Jordan how to cast a rod and reel. He proudly caught a small bass. It was Jordan and I the first night. I'd fixed a covered tent for both of us to sleep under. It rained and cooled things off. The next day Pastor Larry and others joined us. We fished, swam, and hiked and had a really good time, especially cooking out.

From August 20thtoSeptember 3, 2005, six of us went to Hawaii for a super vacation. Sue and I, Ronnie and Marti, my sister Raedene and her husband Darral. The four of us left Tulsa on Saturday, August twentieth flew to Houston where Raedene and Darral joined us on the long flight to Honolulu. Then we changed planes in Honolulu and flew to Hilo on the Big Island of Hawaii. We rode a shuttle from Hilo to Kilauea Military Camp, KMC, arriving at 7:20 p.m. They put us in a large four-bedroom, two-bath house with fireplace, kitchen, and Jacuzzi. Plenty of room and near the dining hall and wash-a-teria. We ate that night just before 8 p.m. closing. Everything we needed we just charged it to our room and paid the whole thing when we departed.

On Monday, we got on the Volcano Chain of Craters Road tour. We took lots of pictures, especially the lava fields. On Tuesday, we did the Hilo Tour, visiting an orchid flower farm, basket weaver and each of the girls bought one, Banyan trees, coconut trees, flowers galore. On Wednesday, we took the Circle Island Tour: Blue water beaches, black sand beaches, native villages, palm trees, sea turtles on the beach, volcano winery, coffee beans growing and drying.

We soon went back into Hilo and rented a minivan, and expanded our tours, went shopping, and went on a snorkeling cruise. Ronnie went out several times to try and get near the lava flow, but the Park Rangers were there to stop you. He went out one morning at 3 a.m. and just barely got close enough to see the fire and feel the heat. All in all, the Big Island is very scenic and interesting. We left KMC on September first and flew back to Honolulu where we stayed two nights in the military's Hale Koa Hotel right on Waikiki Beach. The place had a Base Exchange Store and more. We had reservations that first night for the Hale Koa Luau on the most beautiful setting under the stars in a garden oasis by the sea. The menu included delicacies such as Lomi-lomi salmon, Kalua pig, teriyaki beef, shoyu chicken, Mahi-mahi, fresh fruit, pineapple, and poi. The native food, poi, was terrible. In Texas I wouldn't feed it to my hogs. They also served other food that was much better. We swam on Waikiki Beach. We took a dinner cruise and had dolphins escort us. On the last day we took a tour of Pearl Harbor and saw the Memorial Monument and the sunken U.S.S. Arizona."

About December 6, 2005, we received word from my sister Raedene, that our brother Larry had heart failure and was air-evacuated to a Houston hospital from his home in El Campo, Texas. The next day, December 7, 2005, he died. His wife Barbara was hysterical and didn't know what to do. She had no money and requested help. Our advice was to have him cremated there in Houston. At first Barbara said no, but later after she had time to think about what and how to take care of her responsibilities, she did have him cremated. We sent her 200 dollars for his funeral expense and memorial service. I could not attend his memorial service because I was hospitalized in the VA Muskogee Hospital.

I became ill on Wednesday, December 14, 2005. I began throwing up and had diarrhea. We assumed it was some type of intestinal virus. I continued with both through the day and night on Wednesday and Thursday. On Friday morning, December sixteenth, I had begun experiencing severe pain in my stomach and became concerned that it was more than just a stomach virus. I went to the VA clinic in Tulsa as a walk-in patient and was seen by my regular doctor, Dr. Bonnie Ashing. After describing the course of my illness to her, she seems to agree that it was a virus and prescribed Promethazine HCL twenty-five mg. She also had me lay down on the examining table and made a cursory check of my vital signs. She commented on how distended my stomach was and listened and prodded, but did not seem overly concerned. This seemed strange, given my history of diabetes, and the problems I had with my kidneys in September of 2004.

I went back home and began taking the prescribed medication. However, as soon as I would take a pill, I threw it back up. This continued for several hours. Finally, about 8 p.m., this vomiting seemed to stop, as did the diarrhea. On Saturday morning, December seventeenth, I had a small glass of grape juice. That seemed to stay down so about forty-five minutes later I had another small glass. Shortly afterward, I began vomiting again. By this time, after vomiting non-stop for more than three days, there was nothing in my stomach and I was vomiting greenish black liquid.

It was increasingly apparent that there was something seriously wrong, and since the VA clinic in Tulsa is not open on weekends, we went to the VA hospital in Muskogee at noon on Saturday.

I was seen by the Urgent Care doctor on duty, Dr. McKay, X-rays were ordered, along with other medical tests, blood work, urinalysis, etc. The decision was made to admit me to the hospital. I was almost dehydrated and becoming increasingly weak, and an IV was started to administer fluids.

The next day, Sunday, I was seen by a female doctor, don't remember her name. She ordered an NG tube to be inserted to pump off the liquid that had built up in and around my stomach. She also started me on Zantac for my stomach. She said I needed to be seen by a surgeon, because some type of bowel obstruction was suspected.

On Monday, the surgeon, Dr. Thomas Ward, and his assistant, a PA by the name of Blair, came in to talk to me and my wife. Dr. Ward indicated that surgery would most likely be necessary, but he wanted to wait a day or two and see if the blockage would loosen and pass on its own. That did not happen and on Thursday, December twenty-second, at 1:00 p.m., I was taken to surgery.

The surgery lasted approximately two hours. No blockage was found.

Neither did they find cancer or anything else intrusive. Dr. Ward suspected it was possible Crohn's disease. They took many pictures and lab samples to further study the problem. However, Crohn's was later ruled out by an internist and those studying the lab results.

After surgery, I was taken to ICU where I stayed for the next seven days. was finally moved to the regular floor on Thursday, December twenty-ninth, where I remained until my release from the hospital on Monday, January 2, 2006. The discharge diagnosis was Inflammatory Bowel Disease.

I returned to the VA hospital on January tenth to have the staples and stitches removed.

Since January 10, 2006, my recovery seemed slow. I was very weak, and my appetite was low. I ate a minimal amount of food, yet my stomach and legs were swollen, and I weighed more than I did when I was in the hospital. On January 18, 2006, I was seen by Dr. Thomas Madaj, M.C., Adult Medicine, Hillcrest Medical Group in Tulsa. The lab work was done, and Dr. Madaj prescribed Cholestyramine, and referred me to other specialists.

On January 31, 2006, I was seen by a Nephrology Specialist, Dr. Thomas C. Kenkel, a kidney specialist who first treated me when I was hospitalized in September 2004. Blood lab work was done, and Dr. Kenkel said that my kidney function was deteriorating. Creatinine was 4.1, hemoglobin was 8.8, liver function was OK, potassium was 5.8. I was severely anemic. At that time, Dr. Kenkel ordered a 24-hour urine collection and did an ultrasound of my kidneys. He then prescribed Ciprofloxacin for lung congestion and Procrit to treat anemia. Follow-up lab and an appointment with Dr. Kenkel on February 28, 2006 revealed improvements of all the above functions. Appointments with Dr. Kenkel have been every three months and he ordered me to continue the weekly Procrit shots.

In October 2005, my last appointment with the Tulsa VA Clinic eye doctor, a cataract on the right eye was revealed. I was encouraged to have it removed locally, using Medicare, or to call the VA hospital in Oklahoma City to schedule an appointment there, which could take several months. I contacted Dr. Lin Brister, Eye Care for Tulsa and after examination, was scheduled for cataract surgery on December 19, 2005. That appointment was later postponed because I was in the VA hospital in Muskogee from December 17, 2005 to January 2, 2006. Surgery was finally done on February 13, 2006. Follow-up checks on February seventeenth and twentieth indicate successful removal of the cataract.

Dr. Madaj also referred me to Dr. Richard W. Seifert for a colonoscopy and upper GI series. This was done on February 27, 2006 at Hillcrest Hospital. A small polyp was removed, and a sample tissue was sent to the lab. A small amount of irritation was seen in the stomach and a sample was sent for lab evaluation.

Tests were negative. Dr. Seifert ordered x-rays of the small intestines to be done at Hillcrest on March 13, 2006.

Dr. Madaj referred me to Dr. Michael S. Lowe for gallbladder surgery, after x-rays showed gallstones were present. Surgery was scheduled for March 10, 2006 at Hillcrest Medical Center.

Since being released from the VA hospital in Muskogee on January 2, 2006, the diabetes had changed. I stopped all insulin shots and no longer take the Acrabose pills. I continue to take two Glipizide pills per day which keeps my blood sugar around one hundred. Also, at Dr. Kenkel's direction, I am now taking four furosemide pills per day to reduce fluid retention in legs and stomach. I also stopped taking Clonidine because my blood pressure continues to drop.

On March 10, 2006, gallbladder surgery was performed by Dr. Michael S. Lowe. He had hoped to do Laparoscopic Cholecystectomy, making only three small incisions—one day recovery. But because of numerous adhesions, he was forced to do a regular surgery requiring a full-size incision. This meant that I had to be admitted to the hospital and was there five days for recovery. My staples/stitches were removed on March twenty-third. This surgery added one eight-inch cut, one quarter-size hole and one five-inch cut to the twelve-inch cut made during the exploratory surgery done by the VA in December and the equally long scar from the Gastropexy, stomach stapling, done in 1979. My stomach now resembles a piece of meat that's been on a barbecue grill. I have at-shirt that says, "Grill Sgt.," Makes perfect sense.

I had a follow-up visit with my kidney doctor on March twenty-eighth. Dr. Kenkel and/or one of his staff visited me four out of the five days I was hospitalized. Dr. Kenkel was very pleased with my progress—kidneys came through the surgery with little or no compromise, anemia is improving thanks to the weekly shots of Procrit. Cost of these shots is 309.84 dollars each, of which I pay two dollars and twenty-five cents. Thank God for insurance! I am to continue taking the shots until at least May sixteenth. The Procrit comes through the Wal-Mart Pharmacy in Lake Mary, Florida and is shipped FedEx in a Styrofoam ice chest.

A small intestine x-ray was scheduled by Dr. Richard W. Seifert for March thirteenth, but was cancelled because I was in the hospital. It was rescheduled and completed on March twenty-first. The four hours of x-rays revealed no problems with the small intestines.

Follow-up on cataract surgery on March twenty-first revealed good success. New glasses were ordered and received on March twenty-third. Eyesight is good with new glasses. Follow-up appointment with primary care physician Dr. Thomas Madaj was on April fourth. Dr. Madaj was very pleased with the progress shown. He suggested I take Zyrtec for allergies causing runny eyes and nose. He also suggested Citrucel to soften and loosen bowels. He will refer me to a dermatologist to remove several cancer-type skin growths. For a long time, I have complained to doctors concerning congested lungs. Finally Doctor Madaj got me an appointment with the Pulmonary Section at Hillcrest Hospital. As a result of this test they have concluded that I have COPD, Chronic Oppressive Pulmonary Disease, which is a congestive like Asthma. They prescribed inhalers and now

I have relief, but there is no cure. I now inhale Symbicort twice a day.

From April 27-29, 2006, Sue and I joined with E.L. and Ann Simpson in Branson, Missouri for attendance at the Spring 2006 Jubilee Conference. We shared a condo apartment with the Simpson's. It rained a lot while we were there. The location of the conference was the Tri-Lakes center. Features keynote speaker was David Jeremiah and guests were the pianist Dino Kartsonakis and many others giving their Christian testimonies. A real enjoyable trip. I was really blessed.

From June first through June 13, 2006, six of us, Garland and Sue, Ronnie and Marti, and Darral and Raedene, took a European vacation. Our primary destination was Edelweiss Lodge and Resort in Garmisch, Deutsch, Germany, which is on the edge of the beautiful Bavarian Alps. Each of us three couples traveled separately. Sue and I flew to Detroit, then to Amsterdam, Netherlands, and Munich. Raedene and Darral left DFW to Toronto, Canada, to Munich. Marti and Ronnie flew to Chicago, and on to London, England. From London they took a sleeper train to Brussels, to Berlin, and on to Munich. Sue and I arrived at the Munich airport about two hours before Raedene and Darral arrived. We waited for them and then took a train, twenty miles, to the downtown Munich Central train station where we had a confirmed booking at Hotel Mark, just one block away.

That evening and night, we went sightseeing and eating, *"sehen,"* and having some good German beer, (ein bier bitte). Also, that evening, Darral and Raedene took the train and rented a minivan from Hertz. The next morning, Ronnie and Marti arrived by train from Berlin. We loaded the van and went looking for a place to park near the world-renowned Glockenspiel when all the clocks and ding-dongs went off.

We worked our way out of Munich and drove the fifty-six miles to Garmisch and located Edelweiss Lodge that was our home for the next ten days. During the first full day at the lodge, we drove, rather Darral drove almost every day, to Germany's highest mountain, the Zugspitze. We took the cog wheel train to the top. That alone was very interesting to observe. The ground temperature where we parked was seventy degrees, and when we got to the top, it was snowing, and the temperature was minus six degrees. Cold, strong wind was also blowing. From the top, we experienced inspiring views toward Austria, Italy, Switzerland and Germany.

We ate, drank, and shopped in almost every town that we drove through. We were always on the lookout for restrooms, "Wie komme ich zu toiletten?" One place was Walchensee, Germany. The lake there was beautiful. We saw the Winter Olympic Stadium in Partekirchen, which is Garmisch's sister city, the site of the 1936 Winter Olympics. We spent a full day in Mittenwald, Germany. The town, Mittenwald is a beautiful model city. No cars are allowed in the downtown shopping area. I found it interesting that the city has a man-made concrete trench below the sidewalk with clear running mountain water from melted snow. Mittenwald is considered one of the world's premier violin centers. I talked to a violin maker with the possibility of buying one as an investment, but the bottom dollar was 4,000 dollars.

We took two days and one night away from Garmisch, when we went to Italy. We left early one morning, traveled the thirty-five miles on the autobahn highway system to Innsbruck, Austria to find a place to eat breakfast. We got lost and it was too early-nothing was open. We found a McDonald's and waited in the car until 8 a.m. when they opened. Later on, we got off the autobahn and took an Italian mountain road to Vicenza, Italy where we spent an hour to find Caserma Ederle Army Base. The mountain road was about fifty miles and it was the most interesting and exciting ride that I have ever been associated with. The Army base was heavily secured, but we passed all inspections and the lodging office gave us a three bedroom apartment with two baths and a kitchen and several televisions. We had lunch in the PX and did some shopping. Marti went to the computer room and they closed at 5 p.m. Marti rushed out leaving her purse. Before we could file a lost item with security, they had already contacted us in the apartment. We went and picked it up and everything was intact, including money and insulin. We ate supper, and the next day breakfast from the base Burger King.

We left Vincenza early and had a tough time following the roads to Venice. We got there, parked and rode a boat taxi to the floating city of Venice. There are no automobiles, or roads in the City of Venice, a very crowded area with people and pigeons. The six of us road on a gondola through the Venetian canals, propelled by a single paddle, or oar at the stern. It is amazing how fast they can go and make the corner turns with perfection. We had a very good time and made the trip back much faster by staying on the autobahn. An interesting thing is noted that there are no out-of-country security or check points and, for the most part, no signs telling you that you are entering Italy, Austria, Germany, or Switzerland or wherever. We were hungry as we got back to Partenkirchen and we found this nice Italian restaurant and had some good food and beer, "ich bitte die sehen-hahn beer."

One day we visited Neuschwanstein Castle, often referred to as "the Disney castle." Also, the Linderhof Palace and Herrenchiemsee Castle. We shopped in Oberammergau and Weilheim, Germany. We found a Wal-Mart store in Weilheim. Then on another day, we drove through Liechtenstein on our way to Zurich, Switzerland. We ate lunch in a small cafe in St. Gallen, Switzerland. We shopped in Zurich and on the way back, Ronnie drove, and we found this autobahn highway that took us through a fifty-mile tunnel in Austria.

On another day, we took the horse and carriage ride through the residential and historic section of Garmisch. On this ride was a young Army Chaplain, his wife and son. He was on R&R from Iraq. A few days later, they were in the outdoor Jacuzzi with us.

One day after, we were leaving Neuschwanstein Castle, we were desperately looking for a place to eat and as we were going through Schwangau, or Unterrichten, Germany, we passed by a street that looked like a party was going on out in front of a grocery store. A train had stopped, so we did a U-turn and went back to see what was going on. We found out that the grocery store was having a promotion gathering. Out doors were vendors selling grilled chicken, grilled steaks, beer and pop. Indoors were different food samples, free, and there were picnic tables, so we chowed down, and it was all good food. Beer was SOC a glassful.

Next to the last day there, we took a trip to Salzburg, Austria. We shopped and ate until we got tired. We saw awesome buildings, perhaps where the movie *the Sound of Music* was filmed. We saw Mozart's memorial.

On the last day, we checked out of Edelweiss Lodge and drove toward Munich. We located the Regent Park Hotel in Hallbergmoos, Germany which was near the airport. Sue and I, and Darral and Raedene checked into the hotel, then we drove to the Hallbergmoos train stop, and we all got aboard and went to Hauptbahnhof which is Munich's central train station. We left Ron and Marti because they left later that day by train to Paris, France. The other four of us got back on the train, back to the car parked at the Hallbergmoos train stop. We then made a dry run to the airport. The next day, Tuesday, June 13, 2006, Darral and Raedene took us to our departure depot, then they returned the rental car and went to their departure depot. Sue and I had some extra time in Amsterdam, Netherlands for more shopping, then on to Detroit, and back home to Tulsa. Even in Amsterdam, they, "sprechen sie Deutsch," a language of my ancestors.

From June twenty-ninth through July 1, 2006, I went to my Texas kin and friends. The first night, I spent with my brother John and his wife Barbara, in their Belton resort home near Lake Belton. They took me to a buffet restaurant for supper. The next day I visited with sister Carol and later that evening, I took my other sister, Raedene, and her husband, Darral, to Marlin where we ate in a Mexican restaurant that I had never seen before. Saturday morning, I went to Louis Zaleski's early to visit and show them our Germany trip pictures and that was the day of the annual Zaleski Fish Fry. It's always the best fish fry, probably because Louis knows how to mix up the batter that makes it so delicious. And everyone else brings their favorite pot luck dish to go with the fish. Louis' sister, Marjorie, from Lake Jackson, Texas, always makes a big pot of shrimp gumbo. One year, maybe twenty years ago, I invited my friend Billy Kemp and his now deceased wife, Marilyn, to the Zaleski fish fry and someone brought cooked mini-ears of sweet corn, maybe three or four inches long, and I ate at least twenty ears, but Billy ate them all night, perhaps thirty or forty ears. That's testimony that they were really good. If we hadn't eaten so much fish, we could have probably eaten more.

On October 5, 2006, Sue and I traveled to Bryan and College Station, Texas.

We went sight-seeing and shopping. We stayed in a nice motel adjoining Texas A&M University. We found out that this college ranks among the top four largest universities in the U.S. When we were there, the football team and fans were out of town, yet we found some of the busiest streets, traffic, in the world. Friday night, we were booked to dine and stay at the Sand Hill Ranch, just west of Rockdale, Texas, the home of William and Sheree Smith, my niece, and their two children, Victoria and Wyatt. We left early Saturday morning and visited Darral, Raedene, Carol, and John. Darral had just been released from a Temple hospital, due to a leg inflammation and swelling. Later, we went to my high school for our annual homecoming program and lunch. We left in time to pass through Dallas before the OU and Texas football game ended and got back home to Tulsa about dark.

Our next event was a fall cruise in New England and Nova Scotia. We left October 21, 2006, from Tulsa by air via Cincinnati to Logan Airport in Boston. Our cruise aboard the Jewel of the Sea, of the Royal Caribbean Line, departed from the Boston Port at 5 p.m. that day. During the five-day cruise, we had three stops.

On October 22, we were in Portland and Kennebunkport, Maine. We disembarked in Kennebunkport for lunch and shopping. Sue had boiled lobster and I had fried oysters and a lobster burger sandwich. Kennebunkport is a very beautiful city on the Atlantic Ocean side of Maine.

As we sailed northward, our next stop was Bar Harbor, Maine. It was raining. I sat in the pier dock a long time while Sue went shopping. After she returned, she bought some trolley car tickets, secured her packages in the office, and we walked up the hill to a restaurant and Sue had boiled lobster, and I had fried oysters and clam chowder soup. Afterward, we walked farther up the hill and waited in the rain for the trolley car ride. After our Bar Harbor tour, we asked the driver to let us off in front of the pier and boarded a small boat that took us back to the cruise ship.

Our final excursion was on Tuesday, October twenty-fourth, at Halifax, Nova Scotia, Canada. We arrived at a heavily secured pier with lots of vendor shops. Our excursion was a big bus tour of the city of Halifax. I don't remember much about the tour except no one on the bus chose to get off the bus at each point of interest the driver was trying to convince us to see or pay more money like a museum stop. After getting back to Pier twenty-one, and all the vendor shops, I sat and waited as Sue shopped them all. Upon return to the cruise ship, I just made it in time because I got sick and it came out of both ends with a lot of air pressure each time. We ordered room service meals and never left the cabin that night, because I was in and out of the bathroom throughout the night and the next day. We were at sea anyway. We returned to Boston harbor on Thursday morning.

The flight to Cincinnati was hectic, as I barely made it to the Cincinnati Airport restroom for a big and final blowout excursion. In Cincinnati, we paid twenty-five dollars each for an earlier flight back to Tulsa. We got home before dark, compared otherwise to a 10 p.m. arrival.

Sue was chosen to find and direct another church drama play. So, on March third and fourth 2007, the drama team, after much practice, presented, "The Good Veronican," a dinner theater performance. I was Publicity Director. Will Rogers United Methodist Church's Senior Pastor, David Burris, played the character Abraham, Dr. Mel Whittington, WRUMC Associate Pastor, was the Mayor, Associate Pastor Cyndi Tillery was Master of Ceremonies, Kendall Johnson was Romeo, and Candace Grimes was Juliet, the two later married. The proceeds went to the VIM Mission Fund—very gratifying and successful.

From April twenty-second through April 29, 2007, four of us went on the Royal Caribbean cruise ship, The Explorer of the Seas, for a seven-night Western Caribbean Cruise. John and Michele met Sue and me aboard the cruise ship in Miami, Florida. Jon and Michele upgraded our room to a Junior Suite which included a walk-out balcony. Our first excursion was in Belize City, Belize. We had a horse and carriage ride through town. Our second excursion was Costa Maya, Mexico. Sue and I got a massage on the beach. The next stop was Cozumel, Mexico.

Because of the strenuous walking involved, I stayed aboard and went to the hot tub while the others shopped in town, ate lunch, and took a walking tour. Our last stop was Georgetown, in the Grand Cayman Islands, near Cuba. Sue and I went on a glass-bottomed boat ride. It was great! We saw all kinds of tropical fish. The water was perfectly clear. Then we got on a tour bus and went to *Hell* and back. The city of Hell even has its own post office. The completed cruise was wonderful!

In June 2007, we had some quality time at the church cabin on Ft. Gibson Lake. Our families plus my sister, Raedene, and hubby, Darral, enjoyed the cool breeze and water. We barbecued and had fried fish and a lot more. Cat-fishing was fabulous. The kids as well as the adults enjoyed a continuous burning campfire, lots of burnt wieners and marshmallows.

In September 2007 the four of us, me and Sue, Ron, and Marti, went on a westward vacation. We drove our 2004 Town and Country Chrysler. The first day we drove as far as Albuquerque, New Mexico and got lodging at Kirtland AFB for

Thirty-seven fifty per room. The next day we drove on to Sedona, Arizona and spent two nights in La Quinta Inn. While there, we rode the Verde Canyon Railroad Starlight ride. I got sick and had to throw up in my Air Force ball cap. On Sunday, we visited the South rim of the Grand Canyon National Park. I was still sick to my stomach. We spent the night in the Red Feather Lodge, near GCNP. While Ronnie drove the next day to the scenic north rim of the Grand Canyon, we three stayed at Jacob Lake Inn Gifts and food. I stayed in the restroom quite a lot. Then we drove on to St. George, Utah, where we stayed in the Ramada Inn and shared a large sixteen-ounce steak at Ruby River Restaurant. The next day we left St. George and went back and drove through Zion National Park in Utah. We saw some interesting layers of different rock formations and tunnels.

From September 11-16, 2007, we stayed with Chris and Rena in their Salt Lake City home. The water pump went out on the van and we had it fixed at a firestone store on Saturday. Afterward, we visited the Mormon Tabernacle Choir, the Great Salt Lake, a copper mine, and we went on to the Olympic Park, north of Salt Lake City. After we left Salt Lake City, we traveled the scenic route to Colorado Springs, where we got lodging at the Air Force Academy. The next day, we took the scenic route of Colorado, through Dodge City, and Garden City, Kansas, then on back home to Tulsa.

We curtailed Christmas of 2007 for the adults because we all, twelve of us family, used our gifts for each other for the five-day cruise from Galveston, Texas, and on the Carnival Cruise Lines. Scott and Lisa, as well as John and Michele, flew to Houston. Six of us, including Sue and I, Glenn and Penny, and Troy and Amanda, drove our white Town and Country. John loaned us his covered top carrier. My sister, Raedene, and hubby, Darral, drove to Houston from Lott and met up with my Christian niece, Karol Keno, and her son Robert. We all finally met in Galveston. We all ate dinner in a fabulous restaurant on the beach in Galveston. We twelve departed on Monday, January 8, 2008 on Carnival's fun ship, the Ecstasy. We had two stops, one in Progresso,

Yucatan and one in Cozumel, Quintana-Roo, Mexico. I rented a motor chair to use on board. While at Progresso, we all went to the Corona Beach party. We had lots of beer, other drinks, and snack food galore. It was a beautiful, sunny day. Sue got a massage right there on the beach. Back aboard the ship, we chose to have the semiformal dinner, every evening. They put us at two adjoining tables, six each. One night, we had lobster and all of us asked for seconds. We had some fabulous meals. Eight of the twelve were virgin cruisers and they thought they were in heaven's paradise. They were right. God gives us the desires of our hearts when we seek and live His ways.

While we were shopping in Cozumel, Lisa got sick and had to spend that day and the next in bed aboard ship. Raedene got sick on Saturday morning upon our departure. On the way home, the six of us in our car stopped near Fairfield, Texas, and had a fabulous buffet lunch at Sam's Restaurant. I got sick the next day at home, mostly diarrhea. We have lots of family photos from this trip. We will always cherish these mementos. Who do we know that has equaled a family trip like this?

All in all, I consider my health as not good. These are the names of most of the doctors that cared for me in the year 2006. Dr. Ashing, Dr. Ward, Dr. McKay, Dr. Madaj, Dr. Kenkel, Dr. Brister, Dr. Seifert, Dr. Lowe, Dr. Anderson, Dr. Myers, and R.N. Dinsmore, Center for Diabetes Management, Dr. Brister, eye specialist, was the only physician that prayed for me in his office. He did the cataract surgery on my right eye. I can see fine out of both eyes now with glasses. There's one physician that I speak to everyday. He happens to be the one great physician that can really help me. So far as I know, He has not healed me in a way that I can see. His name is above all names, and that is Jesus Christ, my Lord and Savior.

The diabetes blood sugar is too high. I take insulin shots three times a day. I take Glipizide tablets three times a day for diabetes. For blood pressure, I take Furosemide tablets three times a day, Diltiazem tablets once a day, Clonidine tablets once a day, and Terazosin tablets once a day. For cholesterol, I take Simvastatin tablets once a day. For prostate, I take Finasteride tablets once a day as well as the Terazosin tablets once a day. I take Procrit shots once every two weeks for blood anemia.

Physically, I feel weak at all times. Dr. Kenkel said that I won't get better because of my kidneys. They have deteriorated to twenty-five percent usage. I will have to go on dialysis pretty soon. I have to watch sodium and restrict it from my diet because of my kidneys. I am restricted from using sugar because of the diabetes. With the IBD, Inflammatory Bowel Disease, my stomach is always nauseated, and my bowels are irregular. Sometimes I go four days without a bowel movement. Sometimes when I do have a bowel urge, I have five seconds to get to a restroom. Sometimes, I don't get there in time. Today was one of those times. My anus does not have the strength to hold it back very long. It happened at church one time. Thank goodness there were no witnesses because it took a long time to clean up, including the hallway. Since 1993, my right shoulder, neck, arm, and hand are always in pain. Since 1966, my lower back is always in pain. Sometimes I have to stop what I'm doing and sit a spell to soothe the pain in my back. This is why the D.A.V. gives me one hundred percent disability pay. I can't sleep in a regular bed, because of the discomfort to my back so that's why I have been sleeping in a comfort chair for the past five years.

Both feet are always half numb from diabetes. If I don't take six Furosemide, water pills, a day, my legs would break out in water blisters and after they burst, it becomes a sore that usually takes sixty days to heal. The skin on my arms is tender and bruises quite easily and takes a long time to heal. Another problem has occurred in the past year and that is eye and nose watering. I carry four handkerchiefs everywhere I go. Each morning my nostrils and throat are stuffed full of mucus. It takes over an hour of honking and blowing to breathe halfway. I don't think I will be able to run and wade a trot line or limb line anymore. When I walk, it's all over the path. My hands shake like a cold whore in church. My body temperature is always cold. Thanks to my beloved wife Sue for the past forty-five years, life has been worth living.

This section of my book tells of hemodialysis. On or about August 26, 2008, I was admitted to Hillcrest Hospital due to kidney failure. I was assigned a room and, when I checked in, there was my Assistant Nurse, Melody Cuthbert, from our church. The next day, August 27, 2008, I was wheeled down the hall on the fifth floor of Hillcrest Hospital for my first four-hour ordeal with Dialysis. During this period, which included my seventy-second birthday, I was infested with arthritis in both knees. I couldn't walk and could not move from my chair to my bed that was only two feet away.

After I was discharged from Hillcrest Hospital, I was assigned regular tri weekly dialysis with Central Tulsa Dialysis Center, at 1124 S. Saint Louis Avenue, Tulsa, Oklahoma 74120-5413. I was scheduled every Monday, Wednesday, and Friday, shift one which was 8:00 a.m., for fours hour each day. Some of the staff at Central Tulsa were Brenda, Sharon, Angela, Patrick, Kandis, Caroline, Regina (Grandma), Nathella, Robin, Jana, Susan, Salina, Jennifer, Doug, Ashley, Christian, Stacy, Millie and Kerra.

Last year, 2010, I transferred to Muskogee Community Dialysis, now located at 2316 Shawnee Street, Muskogee, Oklahoma 74401-2283. Between April and September, I came back to Tulsa. Some of the staff there were Angie, Connie, Sheila, Penny, Karyn, Mecie, Malinda, Megan, Anna, Cheri, Tracy and Jeremy. On March 7, 2011 will transfer back to Muskogee Dialysis.

Some of the assigned physicians at both dialysis centers are Dr. Thomas Kenkel, Dr. Thomas Keaveney, Dr. Kusum Bhandari, Physician's Assistant Donna Anderson and Dr. Rajat Kaul.

The dialysis procedure consists of weighing, taking a standing blood pressure reading, then sitting while the blood pressure is automatically taken every few minutes. Temperature is taken in the ear, then two needles are placed in my left arm in the fistula vein, one near the fistula and the other four inches higher away from the first. The nurse or attendant hooks up both needle lines to the dialysis machine. The first tube draws out old blood and it goes through the dialyzer, which cleans my blood like the kidneys normally do, then it returns the clean blood through the upper tube back into my system. At first this was a four hour ordeal, but later Dr. Kaul reduced my time to three and a half hours.

Complications in October 2010 caused this to change my time to three and three- · quarters hours. Upon completion of my dialysis time, they take my temperature and a sitting blood pressure reading, then a standing blood pressure reading and

a departure weight. Failure to pass minimum requirements of any of these requires you to sit or stand until minimum requirements are met.

On March 9, 2009, my friend Carl Cook visited me in the Tulsa dialysis complex. Carl knew of this patient, Marilyn Bartlett, who happened to be Jon Bartlett's mother. In addition to Jon leading the Alpha Group, he was also President of Will Rogers United Methodist Church's Methodist Men. Marilyn has been on dialysis for fifteen years. Marilyn and patient Robert Deer both have fistulas that have caused large golf-ball-sized boils on their arms. On March 13, 2009, I gave Marilyn a copy of this book.

On Wednesday, May 20, 2009, I came home from dialysis and Sue said, "Let's go to the lake" (Ft. Gibson Lake). I had already picked up the keys for both FUMC Bixby and FUMC BA for the weekend, Memorial Day. First, I called our church office and told them that I would not open the church on Thursday morning for the Men's Prayer Group. So we loaded the car and headed for the lake. Both cabins were dirty because neither had been used this year. We checked out both cabins, side by side to the entrance to the UM campgrounds and decided to stay in the first cabin owned by Bixby FUMC. We turned on the power, water, and swept the place and it got cool from two window air conditioners.

We called Michele and Penny and reported our assessment of the quality of the two cabins. Later we ate chicken from KFC Wagoner, then spent the night.

Thursday, we went to Wagoner Wal-Mart and bought gas there for two dollars and eight cents per gallon and then we bought some bait at the bait shop just across the highway from Wal-Mart. We had lunch at Wagoner Sonic. That afternoon I set out twelve limb lines, lake level was nineteen feet above normal and falling and the water was calm. My body strength was below medium. After baiting the lines, we rested and then drove to Choteau and had supper at the Amish Dutch Pantry. The food was delicious, especially the ham that was seasoned and cured just right. We talked about getting one of their hams for Thanksgiving. We returned to Tulsa for the night.

On Friday morning I had dialysis. My blood sugar was 188 so I took a shot of insulin at 1:00 p.m. My body condition was weak. We stopped and bought bait on our way back to the lake. Good thing because the lake dropped over a foot since we were gone and the nice large shiners I had left were above water and dead. At 3:00 p.m. I began to check the twelve limb lines, baited some and rebaited all of them. I put on two waist life jackets and I was wearing my camouflage Air Force cap. The four limb lines nearest the car had on two catfish, and the hook was missing on one of the lines. I began to wrestle with a five pound blue cat. I got him on my stringer, but then I couldn't get him unhooked. I didn't have any pliers with me to assist. I left him on the limb line and tied off the stringer within reach. I pulled off a smaller catfish from one of the other limb lines and put him on the stringer with the big Blue cat. I re-baited that hook and took down the line with the missing hook. The water was wavy, and boats made it even worse. I'm getting weaker and weaker. With bait bucket, I walked the bank to three limb lines that I had to relocate to deeper water. I re-baited six other limb lines, taking off a two-pound catfish and stringing it on my bait bucket. I got back to the car and left this fish tied to a full bucket of water. I was too weak to fight the tree trunks and high waves. I had two new float lines and two other limb lines to bait. I wrestled with one float, trying to get it baited and trying to get it to deeper water. During this time, I experienced leg cramps in my left leg. I would exert a lot of muscle pressure against the cramps to get rid of them. They continually came and went. I was floating in circles and couldn't get a foot grip on the lake bottom since I was out in deeper water. I finally slung out one float line and had as much trouble with the other. I got close to one of the limb lines hanging in a tree, so I grabbed it and pulled my body with it until the line got so tight I had to turn it loose. After about fifteen minutes of bouncing around in circles, I finally got the second float line baited and I slung it out as far as I could.

So now I approach the two remaining limb lines. I baited one and hung on to it until it got so tight I had to turn loose. When I did, the hook caught onto my left hand long fingernail and slung off the bait. So, I paddled around for a long time trying to get back to the waist-deep water where the two limb lines were. At one time, I was so far out that I had to swim back because my feet couldn't touch bottom. After a long dizzy spell of time, I got the last two lines baited, and I started back to where the two fish, one still on line, were strung. I was on my knees near these large tree roots and the car. I struggled to get over these roots with large waves tumbling me to and fro. I took off the line holding the minnow bucket and was able to sling it toward the bank near the car. At this point I thought it might be easier if I released the two life belts. When I did, my body sunk to the water bottom. I was under water a few seconds trying to get my composure. I swallowed some water and lost my baseball cap. It floated away so fast I couldn't reach it. I watched it float away and I made no attempt to retrieve it. I did manage to hold onto the two life belts and slung them to the shore.

While holding onto the tree roots, I managed to crawl out of the water and stand upright. I just stood there leaning against the car for about five minutes. I observed that the catfish tied to the full bucket of water was secure. I got into the car and drove up the hill to our cabin.

It was about two hours later or 5:00 p.m. I changed clothes and shoes, went indoors and book my blood sugar reading. It was sixty-three. No wonder I was going in circles. I ate some honey buns and drank some milk. Gradually I returned to normal senses, except for overcoming dialysis.

Troy's friends and neighbors drove up to the camp. Gregg, Mike, Chrystal, and her two children. Later, I drove over to where they were camping. I asked Gregg to help me. He came over and got the five-pound off and got all three fish on one stringer and he also baited several empty hooks for me. Chrystal's two children's names are Caitlyn and Koal.

About 8:30 p.m., John, Michele, Kenslie, Thomas, Matthew, Penny, Krysta and her friend, Selena Gomez, drove up to join us. All in all, up to Sunday, we caught about forty-five catfish, the largest weighed nine pounds. Then, when John was taking the lines out, he caught a thirty-two pound paddle fish. John pulled out two more catfish and gave them to Gregg and Mike. We had a wonderful Memorial Day weekend (see photo #14).

By the way, I retrieved my baseball cap the next day after losing it. It was three feet on the shore.

During this trip, Kenslie and the other two girls found and claimed a little calico kitten. They wanted to bring this kitten back to Tulsa, but we all said no no-no. On many other trips to the lake, they always managed to find this cat and they named it Kenkie (see photo #15).

Sometime in June 2009, Sue and I drove back to the lake. We were looking at lake property to buy. We have always been fond of this old house rotting on the corner, facing the lake, just north of the Toppers' two stores. We stopped at the all-volunteer Fire Station in Toppers, a suburb of the City of Wagoner. A volunteer happened to be at the station when I got there. I asked this person about the corner lot that we were interested in. He said it belonged to such and such, an old man set in his ways, and that he would never consider selling the place. Okay. We drove around the properties adjoining the Methodist Campground. We found an empty house and went next door and talked to the neighbor. He said that the property was tied up in the courts. So, we drove three houses south and found one with FISBO, For Sale by Owner, out front. The address was and is 72148 S. 323 Avenue. We called the number on the sign. It was Danny F. and Janie M. Wilfong, who now live in upper Alabama.

They were both real estate agents. They left custody of the house to a neighbor to the north, Lynnette Sischo. Lynnette showed us the house. The Wifongs were asking 135,000 dollars. We wrote up a contract and they accepted a sales price of 132,500 dollars. Additionally, we purchased many items coming to 500 dollars. Tulsa Federal Credit Union carried the mortgage of 125,000 dollars at five point five percent, a fifteen-year fixed purchase. We paid 1,500 dollar a month, of which 1,115 dollars was required. We got the house, closed, on July 7, 2009.

In October 2010, we refinanced the Lake House. We closed our savings from Edward Jones Investments and put 33,000 dollars more down, so our new loan was 82,000 dollars for fifteen years at three-point seven five percent adjustable with a first possible increase after three years. Total adjustments could never go over seven-point seven five percent. The effective date of this new mortgage is December 1, 2010.

Since July 7, 2009, we have completely refurnished the outbuilding now called the Bunk House. The cost has been over 4,000 dollars. This includes water and sewer hookup, hot water heater, outside shower, electricity changes, gas line, and cable TV line, new ceiling, rest room, and bunks to sleep twelve or more people. A pool table was included with the property, but we have added a ping pong table on top of the pool table. We have also added a two-car carport with shed space. Cost of this is about 700 dollars (see photo #15). Then, the best increase is a very large deck with sunken hot tub out back facing the lake. Troy designed the deck and he and John built it during the summer of 2010. The cost came to over 5,000 dollars. We just moved our hot tub from our city home in Tulsa to the deck (see photo #16). Last year I had a fairly large garden that required a lot of work but was very fruitful. The size of the garden space is forty-five by seventy-five feet. This year, Scott has loaned us his commercial tiller. Additional expenses have come to over 3,000 dollars, which includes a new, battery-operated golf cart. We all enjoy riding this golf cart, which compares to most residents in Toppers (see photo #16). One planned project for 2010 includes a huge barbecue grill with rotisserie. Later this grill will provide smoke for a six by six by twelve foot smokehouse. Then an asphalt covered circle drive in front of the house.

About the second week of September 2009, we returned for our second trip to Hawaii, however this time Carl and Sue Bennett were with us and we kind of serve as escorts for them, even though we did take a new route. We flew to Los Angeles and from there to Honolulu. We booked the first night again in the Hale Koa Hotel on Waikiki Beach. The next morning, I took a taxi to a dialysis center in southeast Honolulu and had my treatment there. Afterward, I rode the same taxi back to the Hale Koa Hotel where I met up with the Bennett's and Sue. We ate some lunch and then, with all our luggage, we headed to the port and prepared to board ship. The next day we arrived at the port of Kahului at the

Island of Maui. Carl rented a car and we all got on the road toward Hana. We stopped near Keanae, and observed the South Shore waves breezing in. Later we turned around somewhere near Waialua Lookout and took Sue Bennett back to the ship because she was sick. So, Carl, my wife, and I headed south to Ulopalakua where we stopped and had lunch, bought some wine and observed a very large tree that had avocado on its branches. We drove around looking for sights to see. We got back to the ship and the four of us had a nice evening meal. The last thing I remember eating was a lime ice cream sherbet. I got sick after this and had to stay in my room near the toilet. I was still sick the next day but Carl drove me to their dialysis center and I managed a three-hour session. Sue stayed aboard ship while Carl and his wife drove over to Lahaina and shopped. Upon return to ship, I remained sick. About 5:00 p.m. Sue took me down to their Infirmary, and it was full, some throwing up right in front of us. The whole ship was quarantined, especially the dining facility. The doctor checked me over and (Photos #16) said that he couldn't take care of me. He told Sue to go pack a small suitcase and gave us fifteen minutes to depart ship since it was sailing in fifteen minutes. They got me an appointment at Maui's Memorial Hospital. They called a cab for us. They wheeled me off in a wheelchair and they were in a hurry to return the chair back aboard ship. Sue and I set waiting in the Cab as we watched the ship pull away without us.

The cab soon picked us up and immediately the emergency room technicians and doctor at Maui Memorial Hospital checked me over. First, they put me on an IV, then sent me to x-ray, and many other check points in the hospital. After two hours on an IV, I had no fever and I was feeling better. The doctor, John Mills, dressed in blue jeans and tennis shoes, talked to us and said that he was releasing me.

So, Sue called a cab and we went to this motel that the former cab driver recommended to us. We bought some light food and went to bed. The next day we got another cab that took us to the airport. We had a nice, short flight to Hilo's airport on the big island of Hawaii. Carl had just departed the ship and rented a car. He picked us up and we four were back together again. All we missed was the night ship ride from Maui to the big island of Hawaii. Days later, we were reimbursed for all our expenses.

With the rented car, we decided to take the Volcano Chain of Craters Tour.

We visited the orchid flower farm again. We saw all the volcano fields but the Chain of Craters Road was closed halfway around so we came back. We took the Craters Road down to the East Rift Zone as far as we could. The live volcano wouldn't let us get any closer. We viewed the rock shore about fifty feet above sea level. It was very windy also. We had lunch near Wal-Mart in Hilo. Later, on the way back, we attempted to tour the Macadamia nut facility near Hilo but their rooms were full of visitors and we were running out of time. Carl took us back to the ship and he left to turn the rented car back in.

Sue and I had to go back through checking back in starting with the doctor's office. We had nice meals that night but they were harder to obtain due to all the sickness going on.

That night we left the port of Hilo and passed by the active volcano on the southeast side of the island. The next morning, we docked at Konokohau Harbor and again Carl rented a car. They headed south and let me off at Kealakekua for dialysis treatment. My wife led them to the farthest point south and then some, because they wound up on the Pacific Ocean. They got back up to Highway eleven and preceded to Punaluu where the black sand beaches are and the home of large turtles. They returned later after 4:00 p.m. to pick me up. We did some shopping at Kailua Kona before returning to ship and Carl had to return the rented car.

We sailed that night, and the next day, we landed at Nawiliwili Bay, the Island of Kauai. Carl rented a car. We drove up Waimea Canyon State Park to Waimea Canyon Outlook. While the three hiked up the mountain above 3,400 feet to the lookout, I stayed and observed chickens all over this island.

Somewhere further up the canyon is a Methodist campground. Then we saw Waipoo Falls. At the falls is where we found this couple making hats and baskets out of green leaves. When we reached 4,120 feet above sea level, we had to turn around and come back down the canyon. Getting back on Highway 50, we stopped at Pakala and saw coffee beans on the vine and we bought fresh gourmet coffee. Farther back down Highway 50, we stopped at a town called

Eleele and had lunch at the Wrangler's Restaurant. In their parking lot were trees with large fruit hanging on every limb. We drove around looking at things and passed Koloa, then to Poipu. We parked and walked the streets shopping.

There were ceramic dummies in different stores. We took pictures of us with the dummies. Later, after we got back aboard ship, we went all the way around the island of Kauai. We recognized places we had been before that day. We all agreed that Kauai is the Garden Island. It's really beautiful.

The next day, September 19, 2009, we returned to Honolulu and departed ship on passenger terminal two. Carl rented another car and he took me to Siemsen Dialysis Center by 9:00 a.m. The Bennett's toured Pearl Harbor and my wife walked around shopping. They also went to Mt. Tantalus on Round Top Drive where you could see all of Honolulu, including Diamond Head Crater. The next day, September 20, 2009, they took me up the mountain to see how beautiful the sight is. Then we drove on to mid-Oahu and on to the Dole Plantation. While there, we rode the Pineapple Express. We saw pineapples growing everywhere. We went through their garden and saw much more beauty, looked on (see photo #17).

After leaving Dillingham Airfield, we drove along the north beaches and sometimes we stopped and waded in water and picked up shells. Upon returning to Hale Koa Motel, we took pictures of the beautiful trees surrounding it.

The next day Carl drove me to the Dialysis center and later picked me back up. We went back to the hotel, Carl returned the rental car, and they went swimming at Waikiki Beach, while Sue and I took some time in the hotel swimming pool. Later, we dressed and walked behind the hotel to pre-show events at Germaine's Luau. We had the usual menu, Lomi-lomi salmon, Kalua pig, roasted nearby, teriyaki beef, smoked chicken, Mahi-mahi, fresh fruit, pineapple, and poi. Afterward we stopped by the hotel Base Exchange to buy more stuff.

The next day we left the hotel to get on a Delta flight at the airport. We were not allowed to leave the airplane in Los Angeles but continued on to Atlanta and from there back to Tulsa.

Last year, 2010, my granddaughter wrote the following for a school project:

> "VETERAN'S DAY. I can honor a very special veteran who was there when I was born and helped me through the years...my Grandpa Garland. He is very special to me and I love him. He is a Veteran from the Air Force for twenty years. I love him, and I would like to thank him for that. I love you, Grandpa. Sincerely, KENSLIE MULLINGS."

On October 24, 2009, we four, Ronnie, Marti, Sue and I, while driving our Chrysler Aspen, headed west to visit Chris and Babs. We took the normal route to Denver, and then on to Francis E. Warren AFB in Cheyenne, Wyoming. After leaving Denver, we got on this turnpike highway but couldn't find an exit booth to pay so we kept going. A month later we got a bill in the mail. We spent the night and the next day we made it to Hill AFB, in Ogden, Utah, a place we have been to before. On October twenty-fifth, we made it to San Francisco. From Chris' apartment, we could see the Golden Gate Bridge, and also the Oakland Bay Bridge. Monday morning Ronnie drove me to China Town Dialysis Center but they had a bad water leak. So, the Social Services Director sent me over two miles to the Japanese Dialysis Center. Afterward, the whole group picked me up and we found a place to eat lunch. We fixed spaghetti for the evening meal. But earlier that day we toured Alcatraz. Coming back from Alcatraz, we observed hundreds of seals at Pier 30 of Fisherman's Wharf at the bay near Chris' apartment. Later, the next day, we spent the whole day at Yosemite National Park. We had a picnic lunch. On Wednesday I had dialysis at China Town, water leak all taken care of.

That afternoon we went shopping. Thursday, we went northwest across the Golden Gate Bridge toward Santa Rosa and the wine country. We observed many fields of grapes. The five of us had dinner that evening in a San Francisco restaurant. On Friday, I had my regular dialysis again in China Town. They were all very nice people. That afternoon, Sue and I rode the trolley up and down the San Francisco streets. Then Chris drove us all around the surrounding suburbs to places he had clients and stores. The Bay Bridge was damaged by a cargo ship and they closed all traffic for over a week. When Chris drove us around, he went way south to another bridge that crossed the Oakland Bay to get to parts of Oakland, then he went north to Vallejo and came back across the Golden Gate Bridge to get back home.

Saturday, we traveled all day, getting to San Diego, where we spent the night at the Coronado Naval Amph. Base, a real nice facility backing up to the ocean. Sunday morning, we toured and rode a boat at the Maritime Museum of San Diego. That afternoon we traveled the 354 miles to Phoenix and stayed at Luke AFB in Glendale.

On Monday morning, I was scheduled for dialysis. I left the base housing facility early and headed to the dialysis center but the streets dead-ended and I got lost. The dialysis center called me on my cell phone and they tried to direct me, but I was still lost. After that I concentrated on finding my way back to the base. Hours later I got back to base housing and got the others in the car, and headed to Flagstaff and on to Albuquerque, New Mexico where we, again, stayed at Kirtland AFB, Albuquerque, New Mexico. After we got on base, we had a hard time locating the billeting office. Later we toured the city, later we, again, had a hard time locating our apartment. On the way to Albuquerque, all we saw was hills, rocks and cactus. On Tuesday, November 3,

2009, we had no trouble getting across Texas to Oklahoma and home.

Colored photos show inside the Central Tulsa Dialysis Center. Shown are nurses, Kandis Proctor and Regina (Grandma) Brown. The center has twenty-four chairs and serves three shifts per day, Monday through Saturday. Patients, during their three to four-hour ordeal may read, work puzzles, watch television, sleep, or whatever. This center is managed properly. I never was required to wait in the waiting room. I always entered the facility and went directly to my chair and was online within fifteen minutes (reference photo #18.)

Today, February 8, 2011, in the year of our Lord Jesus, on the day of my youngest sister's birthday, my Aunt Julie, my last aunt—or Dad's sister, one of twelve from the Pelzel family, at the age of ninety-nine years, three months, went to meet our Lord in Heaven. She was in a nursing home in Temple, Texas—the same town, but not the same nursing home, of her sister and my mother years before. She mothered six children—my favorite cousins. May she rest in peace. We will see her in a few years (reference photos #2 and 18).

In March 2011, I transferred my dialysis treatments back to Muskogee. This time I was assigned treatments on Tuesday, Thursday, and Saturday. After one week I was assigned better hours and then, on March twenty-eighth, I was assigned dialysis on Monday, Wednesday, and Friday, my choice days. When I began treatments in early March, I was surprised to have nurse Michelle Matlock working with the Muskogee center for I had her at Tulsa Central and also found out that she lives in Broken Arrow in Indian Springs just west of where daughter Michele lives. The center lacks proper management techniques. I have often waited in the waiting room from thirty minutes to one hour. On-line time is decent, but off-line time is slow.

Our former Pastor David Burris was leaving to become District Superintendent in Woodward, Oklahoma, part of western Oklahoma. Pastor Bob Johns from Vinita, Oklahoma would be his replacement. So, Sue and I went to Vinita United Methodist Church in early March 2010, to meet him and his wife Cherry. We were pleased to have them. They joined Will Rogers United Methodist Church in June 2010. Since then, our church seems to have received a boost in interest and joy in life. We love them.

Life continues to bring about new and interesting things that need to be added to this book. Sometime in March 2011, my niece, Karol Jean Kyno, contacted Larry Roy Pelzel, Jr. via Facebook. She asked him if he was her *long lost* cousin. Since then, there have been other communications between "little" Larry and Karol, and also with Larry's half-sister Sherrie Pelzel, who is married to Jose Ortega.

During 1972, when Larry Jr. was four years old, his mother Sue took him from his father, Larry Sr., and ran off with Larry Sr.'s best friend. He was heartbroken because he and Larry Jr. were together all the time and were very close. We all assumed they were living in Ft. Worth, Texas. Sue's sister, Barbara, who is married to John Pelzel, was not in touch with her relatives. Then one year, Barbara told us her sister had died. We assumed it was her sister, Sue, Larry Jr.'s mother. Not so! Only recently we discovered that Sue is alive and was married to another man but is now divorced and living alone. It was a third sister, Geneva, who had died.

Most of this information came to light at a gathering of eighteen people, including Larry Jr. and his wife, Patty, at a Temple, Texas restaurant, the night of April 2, 2011.

Since 1973, we had lost all contact with Larry Jr. although some of the family had received small bits of information from Sue and Barbara's mother, through the years. After she died, all contacts were severed. We found that Larry Jr.'s birthday is April 17, 1968, not September 9, as we had recorded it.

In June 2011, my wife Sue contacted Larry on Facebook. Larry's wife, Patty, is from Roanoke, Texas, and Larry claims Bedford as his home. Both are near Ft. Worth. Coincidentally, my high school classmate Lillian Broughton, whose husband is John Hutchinson, lives in nearby Euless, Texas. And Larry Jr. works for the City of Euless Parks Department.

Raedene, Darral, Karol, and Robert met "little" Larry and his wife Patty at the Exxon station in Lott. They drove out to the old home place, farm, and then went on to Westphalia, where they visited the old school museum, cemetery, and church. Dennis' son, Joey, and Ricky Montgomery were there as well. Afterward they all went to the Westphalia ball field and had a picnic lunch. At about 4:00 p.m. they all car-pooled to John's house in Morgan's Point where Larry met his uncle John, Aunt Barbara, and cousins, Tammy and Mark, Tammy's husband, Sean, and daughter Sterling. Later, all went to supper at cousin Brent Zaleski's, Maurice's son, restaurant called *Chuck's*. Maria Lewis and kids, Gabrielle and Preston joined everyone there and had a delicious barbecue along with some good fellowship. Officer Jimmy Lewis, Maria's husband who is with the Temple Police Department, stopped by to meet Larry and Patty. Everyone stayed until closing time. NOTE: This information was provided by my sister, Raedene, and her husband, Darral, when they visited us July sixth through twelfth, 2011. We enjoyed their company, especially when Darral and I caught approximately 150 pounds of catfish on just one trotline (see photos #19, 20, 21).

Prior to their arrival on the sixth, Sue and I participated in our church's annual Patriotic Service on July 3, 2011. Sue sang in the choir and I represented the Air Force in the recognition of the individual branches of the Armed Forces (see photo #22: Left to right are Garland, Carl Bennett, John Philips, Doug McBeath, and Ron King.)

We now have plans to take a family cruise from Galveston in January 2012, similar to the one we took four years ago. But this time we are including all of our grandchildren and any other family members who have the funds to go. As of now, there are about thirty-five planning on making the cruise. We depart on January 2 and return on the seventh, with stops in Progresso and Cozumel.

On January 1, 2012, twenty-one of our family and seven from Ron and Marti's family went to Galveston, Texas, for a cruise on Carnival Cruise lines, to Progresso and Cozumel aboard the Triumph ship. We traveled on January first and stayed in Comfort Suites Hotel. While there Karol Kyno and her son, Robert, visited with us in the hotel. The next day I had dialysis treatment in nearby League City before cruise take-off and first thing upon return on January seventh. We all had a good time. One day was a Coronado beach party in Progresso. Sue got a massage right there on the beach. While at Cozumel, all we did was shop and eat.

Starting in 2013, we started having a Pelzel Family Gathering each second weekend of June or one week before Father's Day, at our lake house and church campgrounds, at Fort Gibson Lake in Wagoner, Oklahoma. This gathering only consists of the living descendants of my parents, Johnny R. and Irene M. Boettger Pelzel, both now deceased. We reserve five church cabins and one campground space with electrical hookups plus our house and bunkhouse that sleeps twenty-two people alone of my immediate family. We usually start on Friday evening. On Saturday we have a fish fry and Saturday night we usually cater a meal from Wagoner's Smokin' Sisters Bar-B-Cue. We can drink beer on our property, not the church or lake. We fish, hike, ride our golf cart, play games, sun, swim, sit around a camp fire, talk, and play music until 10 p.m. Everyone usually leaves for home on Sundays...some stay much longer. In 2013 we had thirty-five in attendance. In

2014 we had thirty-nine, in 2015 we had thirty-nine and last year, 2016, we had forty-two. In 2017 it will take place on June ninth, tenth, and eleventh.

In September 2014, Sue and our friends, Sue and Carl Bennett, went on a trip through Illinois and Wisconsin. We left on Friday, September nineteenth with intentions to stop in mid-Missouri and get lodging at the Leonard wood Army Base, but it was early, so we went on through St. Louis and stopped in Beltsville, Illinois and got lodging at Scott Air Force Base. The next day we went on to North Chicago and checked into Navy lodging at the Great Lakes Navy Training Center. Then we went back to Sue's son, Jarrod Hershberger's place, now Doctor Jarrod, visited his apartment and then ate dinner together at a fabulous Chicago restaurant.

So, on Monday I needed to get to Sheboygan, Wisconsin early to have my dialysis. While I was on dialysis, the other three went to see the world's largest flag pole and other sights. Afterward we traveled west to Fond-du-lac, Wisconsin and ate dinner while I was trying to locate my old fishing partner, when we were in the Air Force together at Pagwa River Air Force Station, located on the Pine Tree line in Ontario, Canada. All I remember is the name Tony. I couldn't find him in Fond-du-lac nor could I even remember his last name. I hope to see him in Heaven. So, we went on to Madison, checked into a motel, then we drove around and visited the state capitol.

So, the next day was a full day for we drove fifty miles to Spring Green, Wisconsin to visit the Famous

House on the Rock. This place is beyond anything that a person can imagine. To tell someone about it is beyond comprehension. All you can tell them is that you must see it. We do have a large book to show people what it has, but that's it.

The rest of that day we traveled 664 miles back to Branson, Missouri.

Wednesday, I had dialysis in Branson. We ate a fabulous meal and saw the show "Jonah and the Whale." The two nights there we stayed in Carl's relatives' place called Gwen's Condo. We came back home on Hwy. 412 through Springdale, Arkansas where we stopped to eat at the AQ Restaurant and had their famous fried chicken. We made it on to home on Thursday, after about a 2,000-mile trip. I had dialysis on Friday, my regular schedule.

In 2015, we as a family of twenty-seven people, took a vacation trip to the Gulf Coast beaches in Pensacola, Florida. Since we failed to get Navy lodging, we rented a large house near the beach, costing us nearly 6,000 dollars for the long fourteen-hour trips, one way on August first and return on the eighth. I had three sessions of dialysis while there at Pensacola's Dialysis Center. We had a large family dinner at Peg Leg Pete's Oyster Bar. Lots of Sand-Sun-Surf. One day, we saw the Blue Angels flying exercises. One day there was a float trip down a sweet water river. Matthew caught some waves. A lot of pictures were taken inside the cockpit of a fighter jet. It is written: The sand may brush off, the salt may wash clean, the tans may fade, but the memories will last forever, a God thing.

Since I'm on the subject of vacation, I'll tell about our 2016 Padre Island trip to Corpus Christi, Texas, during July 30 to August 6, staying at the Navy lodging near the beach. Like last year, we drove five cars from Tulsa, and, of course, Darral and Raedene drove their car from near Troy, Texas. We all took the costly toll road around Austin that saved a lot of time with hardly no traffic. Renting five rooms at the Navy Lodge was kind of inconvenient, but the price was much lower. With me being handicapped, it was an experience and I'll explain that later in this book. Our biggest inconvenience was base security. The four of us with military

I.D.s had to escort the other four cars into the base each time. Darral was instrumental in doing a lot of escort time. Thanks, Darral. The same thing happened one day, when we revisited our old house on Randolph Air Force Base. While we were in San Antonio, we all went through the Alamo, went on a boat downtown on the river and walk, went shopping at the Mexican Market, and had dinner at the Mi Tierra Mexican restaurant. Meanwhile, back at Padre Island, John caught some crabs and one night we had steak and seafood for dinner. Both going and coming, we were all impressed at the gas station, food, and gifts business called Buc-ee's near Temple, Texas.

In December 2015, I had my left knee replaced by Doctor Scott Dunitz, from Tulsa's St. John's Hospital. From the hospital I began rehab at Forest Hills Rehabilitation Center and I didn't do very well. I transferred to further rehab at Cornerstone Hospital, located in the Broken Arrow St. John's Medical Facility. My knee got infected so back to St. John's Hospital. The prognosis appeared really bad, perhaps six months of more hospital time. With family, we decided that the best thing would be to have the leg amputated. So, on January 26, 2016, my left leg was cut off above the knee by Doctor Falz Tuma. After a few more days in St. John's Hospital, I was transferred back to Cornerstone Hospital's physical therapy unit, as an inpatient. I received my normal tri-weekly dialysis while there, in my own bed. My leg was healing from the somewhat thirty stitches, but my biggest problem was my butt chapped and hurt all the time, because I could only lay in bed, right side up. I remember one day, after most of the stitches were gone, my grandson Spencer Smith came and rewrapped my stub leg. He is in training to become a nurse or related medical field.

So later in 2016, I was transferred to Kaiser rehabilitation Center at downtown Hillcrest Hospital, as an inpatient. They really worked me hard and I progressed quickly while there. I got around greatly in a wheelchair. We have two house pets, dogs that we love dearly. I missed them so very much. Both are small, about twelve to fifteen pounds. At home we have a doggie door to the back yard and they never potty indoors. Both are females, and neutered. Libby is a Shih-Tzu poodle and sleeps with Sue. Lucy is a blonde Shi-Shon and sleeps with me. Every day, they both want to be held like a baby and they both like to be taken outdoors in front of the house near the street. On about three occasions, Sue managed to bring them to me in the hospital, usually a non-busy weekend. When a nurse came in to take care of me, the dogs would growl.

So, I graduated on February 24, 2016, from inpatient, to home and outpatient status, with a lot of equipment help from All Saints Medical Supply and from my son-in-law, John Collishaw, making our house suitable for an amputee.

I was fitted with a leg prosthesis by Scott Stromberg, CPO, from Hanger Clinic of Tulsa. Since my amputee was above the knee, the artificial leg was and is too hard to master even after many adjustments. Kaiser Rehab finally released me because Medicare Service ran out, and I don't have thousands of thousands, nearly a million dollars to pay a private firm. While at Kaiser Rehab, they trained me very well to move off and on the wheelchair.

I didn't give up. I contacted the Veterans Administration and they set me up for physical training with Team Select, Home Health Care. Twice a week, their therapist, Paul Rumrul, came to my house and worked with me. He continued to work with me until I failed to show any more improvements, and like the other, Medicare wouldn't let him go any longer.

So, guess what? My prosthesis sets in a corner of my closet. I'm comfortable with my wheelchair with a special air pocket cushion. With special ramps, I go with both dogs to the front and back yards, check the mail box, go down the street, stand to brush my teeth, potty with bars and an extended seat, wash dishes, wash and fold clothes, and attend Sunday school and church, go to movies, help grocery shopping, ride in the car for long vacation trips, and live a life, hopefully, pleasing to my Lord, Jesus Christ.

I got sick in May and did more hospital time from May second and May sixth, 2016, at Hillcrest South Hospital. On two different days, they entered my lungs from my back and extracted a quart of brownish fluid from each lung. Problem unknown but healed.

Since then we have changed almost all our doctors to that area of Tulsa. Our family doctor is now Lisa King, M.D., a Christian. For the last eight months I've had this hole in my right leg ankle bone, cause unknown, but I've visited a wound specialist, Doctor Ronald Brown, located at Hillcrest South Medical Building. It's almost healed.

I have a letter from my youngest granddaughter that I want to place in this book. A lot of the information is some of what I have already told in this book, but I really want the reader to visualize in their hearts that I am a Christian created by God, loved by God and by my life style, I try to fulfill God's law to love one another as I love myself.

This is Krysta's letter given to me at Christmas, December 25, 2016 (see "My Inspiration" by Krysta Crawley).

"Ever since I was born, my Grandpa Garland has been the only grandpa I have come to know. He is retired from our U.S. Air Force, and someday I want to follow in his footsteps and join the Air Force! In the past year or so, he has gone through a lot more than I think that I could ever handle when he lost his leg due to a really serious infection in his knee. He still gets through his days, even though he is almost eighty years old now. He inspires me to do great things in my life!

My Grandpa Garland is my mom's dad. I've never known my dad's dad because he chose not to be a part of our lives. But that's okay, that just makes my Grandpa Garland even more important to me! My grandpa has eleven grandchildren in total and I am the youngest out of all of them. I am also one of only three of his grandchildren that is a girl! He is a big part of our huge family and one of the reasons that my family is so close. Grandpa is a major part of our family history. If we were to lose him at this point in our lives, we would all be devastated!

After being in the U.S. Air Force for twenty years, Grandpa Garland retired in 1976. He gets a lot of benefits from his retirement, including discounts during family vacations! It is pretty great because he deserves the benefits that he gets from his retirement. His long years of hard work and dedication in the Air Force, inspires me to maybe one day, do the same as him.

For years, my grandpa has really bad knee problems in his left knee that

restrained him from walking without a walker or some sort of help. Last year he decided to get surgery done on his knee to reconstruct it. After surgery, he was doing okay until he got a serious infection in that knee,

when his incision from the surgery reopened. The infection pervaded through his leg. It got so bad that they had to amputate his left leg from a little above the knee. He went through months of sitting in the hospital and doing physical therapy nearly every single day. Today he still does physical therapy to help with walking using prosthesis.

I have seen Grandpa struggle, I've seen him get frustrated with the process of losing his leg, yet he gets up and gets through all of it day by day even though he is also a diabetic. He never ceases to inspire me. Grandpa turns eighty this month, but I know he still has a lot left in him! He doesn't quit, he just keeps going. I know that sometimes it scares the family that he's getting pretty old in age, but I don't doubt him because he is a fighter.

Grandpa is our fighter!

I hope that one day in the future I can be like grandpa—strong minded, has a lot of will power and never gives up! He knows that he has many reasons to keep going on through his days, even the toughest of days. His family is his reason he inspires each and every one of his family members, I see it in their eyes when they look at him. Most of all, my Grandpa Garland inspires me to do great things in life! Krysta Crawley 2016"

On page 120 of this book, it tells about a Florida trip that we went on in February 2002. We visited my daughter Debbie and my granddaughter Summer Rose. Since I gave Debbie up for adoption to my ex-wife and her remarriage to James Oates, the relationship has always been low key. On this trip I could never dream or think that I would never see Debbie again during this earthly time we have to live. Sometime about 2011, I first found out that she had died on

November 30, 2008. She is probably buried in Slidell, Louisiana. Summer Rose is now 19 years old, and seldom shows much interest in the Pelzel families. See funeral notice from the Orlando Sentinel:

> "HOLDER, DEBORAH "KAY", forty-eight, Clermont, passed away Sunday, November 30, 2008 at South Lake Hospital. She was born May 6, 1960 in Houma, LA, daughter of James William Oates, Sr. & Frances Bergeron. She was a homemaker and a local resident since 1996 from Slidell, LA. She was of Baptist faith. On November 26, 2000 she was united in marriage to Michael John Holder. Surviving is her husband Michael & daughter Summer Rose of Clermont, parents Frances & James Oates, Sr. & siblings Peggy (Gerald) Doucett, James (Shannon) Oates, Jr. & Michael (Lisa) Oates all of Slidell, LA. The memorial service for Kay Holder will be held at 6PM on Tuesday, December 2, 2008 in the Becker Chapel. Kay's brother, Rev. Michael Oates will officiate. Further services and interment will take place in Louisiana. BECKER FAMILY FUNERAL HOME, 806 W. Minneola Ave., Clermont, FL 34711. Telephone 352-394-7121.

Our church has a policy of giving food supplies to the needy. Volunteers are asked to restock the pantry. Recently we were very low on pantry items so they developed a contest for the family that brought in the most canned soup supplies, promising a gift to the winner by February the fifth, super bowl Sunday. Sue and I won the prize of a basket full of super bowl snacks. Over all we collected over 300 cans of soup of which 108 came from us. In the book of Malachi of the Bible it says, "Bring in the full tithes to the storeroom and see if your household can't find room enough to receive the fullest of God's grace." We do on both counts. PTL.

In 2017, from July twenty-eighth through August fourth, we took the whole family to Surfside Beach near Freeport, Texas. There were twenty-one people on this trip. We took five cars from Tulsa, and Darral and Raedene drove down from Troy, Texas, to join us. We rented two beach house, side by side. Everyone shared in preparing meals and general clean-up. On the last night we treated everyone to a seafood dinner in Lake Jackson. I had my favorite, fried oysters. We took one whole day and drove to Galveston, about thirty-five miles away, and did some sightseeing and shopping. I had two dialysis sessions while we were there in Lake Jackson. Everyone said it was a great vacation and we look forward to going back.

In November of 2017, we, as a family, had another life changing event occur which came out of the blue. In October, the kids finally convinced Sue to have her DNA tested to see how much Indian blood she, and they, actually had. As it turned out, she and Marti have none, zero percent, zilch. That came as a big shock because they had been told their great, great grandmother was a full-blooded Cherokee!

But a month later, Sue got a message from Ancestry.com that she had a message from a possible relative on her family tree. When she went online to check it out, this is what she found, in part:

"Hi, my name is Kathryn and you popped up as a possible match, so it looks like we are related somehow. I am actually adopted. I was born on Oct. 19th, 1980, in Tulsa, OK. All I know about my birth mother is that she was about 19, had dark hair and an unusual last name. Would you know any information that might help connect me to my birth family?"

In case you haven't put the pieces together yet, she is the daughter Penny gave up for adoption thirty-seven years ago. Sue responded immediately with a few additional questions just to make sure she was who we hoped she was. And Kathryn sent a current picture which sealed the deal! The resemblance between her and Penny in undeniable!

To say we were all overcome with joy is an understatement! We had all prayed all these years that she would one day look for her mother and be reunited to our family.

In January 2018, Kathryn and two of her best friends flew to Tulsa for a momentous reunion. Penny and Krysta, who had an instant connection with her, took them sightseeing: the Golden Driller, ORU Praying Hands, and a lot more, and everyone gathered here at our house for some wonderful family visits. And we were blessed to host the whole family at Tally's Diner on a Friday evening. It was amazing to watch Kathryn fit in to the family like a missing puzzle piece! We all felt God was smiling and reminding us that our reunions in Heaven will be even sweeter.

Later on, in January, we had a birthday party at the lake house for Jordan and Dalton. Krysta was able to Face Time with Kathryn on her iPad, and everyone was able to talk to her. We even showed her the pictures of her we had added to our family wall and she showed us her house, she lives in Knoxville, TN. It was the next best thing to being with her.

Penny and Krysta and Kathryn have all been in constant touch since then and there will be many other visits in the future. We had offered to pay for an airline ticket for her to come for our Pelzel Gathering in June. But we just recently discovered that Kathryn's adopted mother has Liver cancer, and Kathryn is staying close to home in order to be there for her mom. We are all praying for her family there.

Going back for a minute. I got sick enough on New Year's Day, 2018, I asked Sue to take me to the ER at Hillcrest South. They admitted me with extra fluid around my heart and lungs. They resolved this problem by scheduling me for extra dialysis three days in a row to remove the extra fluid. I went home on January third.

The problems in 2018 continued to get worse. The Oklahoma Heart Institute at Hillcrest has been testing me for a long time through Dr. Matthew B. Good. During late January 2018 OHI scheduled me for an Angio-Seal Vascular Closure Device (TAVR) to be performed by Dr. Kamran I. Muhammad and his staff, including Georgianne Tokarchik, CNS. Surgery at Hillcrest OHI hospital was scheduled for 7:00am on Jan.30, 2018. I'm so glad they put me to sleep, because Sue said I was in ICU over three and a half hours. They found other problems and determined I needed a pacemaker because of slow heart rate. At that point they had to intubate me and inserted a tube down through my nose. But it started bleeding, so they pulled it out and inserted it on the other side and it bled too.

When I woke up, everyone was gathered around me as I coughed up huge amounts of blood and mucous. It took several tries and a lot of time to get the bleeding from my nose to stop. I was not comfortable! After everyone left, I tried to sleep but couldn't and they weren't authorized to give me a sleeping pill. At 4 a.m. I asked to go to the bathroom but couldn't get my bowels to move. I was able to sit in an arm chair the next day. My butt was really hurting. They brought breakfast and I ate some of it. They said I could go home to have dialysis on schedule. Before discharge they did another round of all the tests which they had performed when I was admitted, EKG, x-rays, blood work, ECG, etc.

OK, so I get home about noon and then go to dialysis at 4:00. Got home later and played with our pet dogs, Libby and Lucy, both females weighing about thirteen pounds each. Thursday, I rested as much as I could while still hurting from all the cuts and bruises. On Friday, I made it through the regular dialysis, but it was rough, as usual. More rest while still in pain on Saturday. Skipped church because of the recent flu outbreak. Monday, dialysis again, then an appointment with Georgianne Tokarchik, CNS at OHI for TAVR follow up. I was complaining about weakness and shortness of breath, while she checked me over. She could find nothing but sent me for additional testing and refilled my prescription for antibiotics.

Tuesday, Jan. 6th, I was scheduled for another Echo-Cardiogram, which had been scheduled by Georgianne. Nothing new, no new problems. PTL!

I felt at my worst on Wednesday, Feb. 6, 2018. The next day was regular dialysis. Afterward I went to the dentist, Dr. John Rogers. Later that day, a piece of the crown broke off and pinched under my tongue. After dialysis on Friday, I returned to the dentist's office and a technician repaired the broken temporary crown.

On Thursday, February 1, 2018, my high school buddy, Randall Rhone, called me from his business in San Antonio, and we talked for over an hour, both telling stories from each side. He had just returned from the funeral of friend, Raymond Gregor. Randall said he thought there might have been over 3,000 people there and none were from our home town of Lott, TX, except kinfolk.

Randall shared that his wife, Jimmie, has a pacemaker and recently the batteries went dead, so instead of replacing the batteries, they just replaced the pacemaker with a new one.

The following is my opinion about the life of my friend, Randall Rohne.

We have known each other for more than sixty-five years. I know that through the years he has made many mistakes and done things he probably regrets. We all have! And we've read about many of those same things in the Bible. God's people have always sinned and disappointed Him. Look at King David, he was, "a man after God's own heart," and yet he sinned against God many times. He and Bathsheba even lost their first-born son due to the nature of their sins. But God forgave them.

Randall and Jimmie have both accepted Jesus Christ as their personal Savior and have asked and been forgiven of all their sins. They have built a good life and are continuing to work well into their retirement years, providing employment for his staff and paying taxes to our government. Jesus is continuing to record their good deeds in His Lambs Book of Life in the third heaven, Paradise. When they die or when Jesus comes back, that's where *we* will be and later with God in the New Jerusalem as indicated in Chapter twenty-one of Revelation in the Bible (NIV).

As I near the ending of this book, I will add some precious words for the reader. This, I hope, will save one or many from a life of evil.

"Today is my day for a miracle. I will keep looking up and forward. I am blessed and highly favored by a great God. I will not let negative thoughts occupy one second of my mind. I am secure, sane, and full of joy. I am moving forward. I declare this will be a day of awesome opportunities that will outweigh any and every obstacle that may try to hinder my purpose. I serve an awesome God who walks beside me and blesses me with all good things!"

Jesus said in John 14:14 of the Bible, you may ask me for anything in my name, and I will do it. You must be patient though, as you look for His answer. Don't you think it might take time to manage or handle prayer request immediately for seven or more trillion followers? Keep Jesus Christ in your heart and live a life pleasing to Him. He will promise you eternal destiny. My blessings go with you.

THE END

APPENDIX (Photo I.D.'s)

1. Mom and Dad's fiftieth wedding anniversary
2. Grandpa and Granma Pelzel's marriage
3. Dad's complete family
4. Former Rosebud Hospital
5. Complete Pelzel family when I was eight years old
6. Garland holding twenty-seven plus pound fish
7. Grandson Jordan holding Grandpa's twelve pound fish
8. Mom and Dad's fiftieth wedding anniversary
9. Mom and Dad's sixtieth wedding anniversary
10. Garland holding JESUS sign in March for Jesus Parade in year 2000.
11. Grandpa Boettger, Uncle Roy Boettger, and great grandparents Zoch's tombstones.

12. Grandparents Pelzel's and Great Grandparents Schmid's tombstones
13. Brother Dalton's tombstone, September 2002
14. John Collishaw and Garland holding fish. The paddlefish weighed thirty-two pounds.
15. Kenslie's cat, Kinky, carport and catfish
16. Deck, sunken hot tub and golf cart at lake.
17. Pineapple, and Garland riding in a glider plane.
18. Dialysis center employees and Aunts Julie and Annie.
19. Darrel and Garland's catch of catfish.
20. same thing
21. same thing
22. 2011 Patriotic Service at church.
23. Granddaughter Summer Rose.
24. Granddaughters Krysta Crawley and Kathryn Hallquist

Photo #1
Photo taken in 1980 at Mom and Dad's fiftieth wedding anniversary celebration. At bottom left to right is Grandma Lydia Boettger, Dad and Mom, at top left is Carol, John, Larry, Dalton, Raedene, and me, Garland.

Photo #2
November 9, 1897 Wedding photo of Heinrich & Anna Schmid.

Photo #3
Heinrich (Henry) Pelzel, wife Anna Schmd, and Children
Back row: L to R — Rosie (Hering), Henry Jr., Mary (Dreyer), Alois, Freda (Ballard), Fritz. Front row: Annie (Fuchs), Mrs. Pelzel holding Edward, Julie (Zaleski), Mr. Pelzel holding Ben, and Johnnie. Photo taken in 1917.

Photo #4
Recent photo showing the building that was once Rosebud Hospital.

Photo #5
1944 photo of the Pelzel family, probably taken by Uncle Buster Ballard. Buster's parents and Mr. and Mrs. Becker (Pelzel family friends) are included in this photo. Can you find Garland, who was eight years old in this picture?

Photo #6 and Photo #7
Left picture is Garland holding one day's catch from Lake Ft. Gibson. The large flathead weighed in at twenty-seven pounds! Right picture is Grandson Jordan, at age two, holding Granpa's catch which was a twelve pound Drum.

Photo #8 and Photo #9
Top picture is Mom and Dad at their fiftieth wedding anniversary party. Bottom picture is ten years later at their sixtieth anniversary in 1990.

Photo #10
Garland Pezel carries a sign as he takes part in the March for Jesus on Saturday downtown Tulsa.

Photo #11

Photo #12

Photo #13

Photo #14

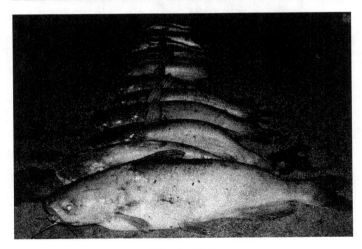

Photo #15

Photo #16

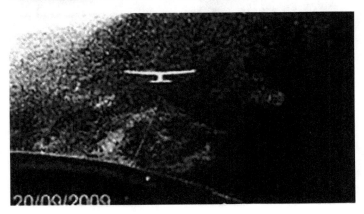

Photo #17

Daughters of Henry Pelzel (1864). Left: Julie Pelzel Zaleski (1911), right: Annie Pelzel Fuchs (1909)
Photo courtesy of James Pelzel, Rosebud, Texas.

Photo #18

Photo #19

Photo #20

Photo #21

Photo #22

Photo #23

Photo #24

CPSIA information can be obtained
at www.ICGtesting.com
Printed in the USA
FSHW010410010619
58619FS